Asperger Syndrome in the Family

by the same author

Pretending to be Normal
Living with Asperger's Syndrome
Liane Holliday Willey
ISBN 978 1 85302 749 9

Asperger Syndrome in Adolescence
Living with the Ups, Downs and Things in Between
Edited by Liane Holliday Willey
Foreword by Luke Jackson
ISBN 978 1 84310 742 2

of related interest

Asperger's Syndrome
A Guide for Parents and Professionals
Tony Attwood
ISBN 978 1 85302 577 8

Living and Loving with Asperger Syndrome
Family Viewpoints
Patrick, Estelle and Jared McCabe
ISBN 978 1 84310 744 6

Freaks, Geeks and Asperger Syndrome
A User Guide to Adolescence
Luke Jackson
ISBN 978 1 84310 098 0

Asperger Syndrome and Long-Term Relationships
Ashley Stanford
ISBN 978 1 84310 734 7

Asperger Syndrome in the Family

Redefining Normal

Liane Holliday Willey

Foreword by Pamela B. Tanguay

Jessica Kingsley Publishers
London and Philadelphia

First published in the United Kingdom in 2001
by Jessica Kingsley Publishers
116 Pentonville Road
London N1 9JB, UK
and
400 Market Street, Suite 400
Philadelphia, PA 19106 USA

www.jkp.com

Library of Congress Cataloging in Publication Data
A CIP catalog record for this book is available from the Library of Congress

British Library Cataloguing in Publication Data
A CIP catalogue record for this book is available from the British Library

ISBN 978 1 85302 873 1

Printed and bound in Great Britain by
MPG Books Group, Cornwall

*To my family – Growing up is only really possible
because I have you all to catch me when I fall.
and
To j – My muse and one of my most precious friends.*

Contents

Acknowledgments

Since finding my way to the AS community, I have been truly privileged to walk beside many wonderful guides, all of whom gave me a few moments of their good will, their good wishes and their good advice. St. Tony Attwood, Pam Tanguay and Susan Richer stand tallest among those folk. My thanks, I give them. The kind souls at Jessica Kingsley Publishers also deserve more appreciation than I can show. They are truly a sweet source of inspiration. Lastly, I offer my aspie friends that place in my heart which will ever hold them as very welcome company and companions.

Foreword

How often have we wanted to climb inside the psyche of our loved one with AS? To understand why they don't say the words we want to hear…I love you…or enjoy an affectionate embrace. Why is it so hard for them simply to relax and go with the flow? We constantly wonder if our children will become independent adults. Will they have a career? Marry? Have children? Are we doing the right things to help them along their path? As parents, we are riddled with questions, and few answers, when considering the future of a child with AS or a related disorder.

Liane Holliday Willey is an accomplished and unique individual. She holds a doctorate degree in psycho-linguistics, is a published author and public speaker, is married, and has three children. What makes her unique is that she also has Asperger Syndrome, as does one of her daughters. Her first book, *Pretending to be Normal*, was a first-person account of what it is like to grow up with Asperger Syndrome. A truly gifted writer, Liane allowed us to see the world through AS eyes: the confusion, the misunderstanding, the sense of bewilderment, which are part and parcel of the disorder, as she grew from child to adult.

The author has written this, her second book, from the perspective of an adult with AS, and courageously shares her private thoughts and fears, and what it means to be married and raise a family when encumbered by a neurological disorder. We see the difficulties of a parent with AS raising a child with the same disorder, but we also learn how challenging it is for a parent with AS to raise neurologically typical children. Liane explains how the many everyday tasks of raising a family often derail her, and how she, her husband, and her children have learned to compensate for the AS that she and her daughter share. The author uses her incredible writing talent, combined with tons of her own special wit and wisdom, to educate - to help us understand *her* world, and the world of others who share her AS.

This is a wonderfully inspiring story, and all the more powerful because it is true. It gives us tremendous insight into what AS adult life might be like for our children, and how to prepare them for independence and intimacy. Liane, her husband, and their children have created a home environment and lifestyle that works for them. Is it what we might consider normal? Who's to say? What is important is that they are happy, each individual's needs are met - they are a family, finding strength from each other. With the telling of her story, Liane has provided us with the gift of insight into living life with AS which will help us better parent our children toward adulthood.

We owe Liane a tremendous debt of gratitude for stepping out and sharing her experiences. She is by nature a very private person, and might have selected a lower profile for herself. But there is her AS daughter. And like any parent, she wants a better world for her child. Understanding will lead to that better world, and with her books and personal appearances, Liane is making a significant contribution to helping us better understand AS.

Pamela B. Tanguay
February, 2001

Introduction

When my oldest daughter was three years old, I bought her a poster showing a rainbow dotted Dalmatian puppy playing beneath the caption, 'Dare to be different'. Little did I know the poster's message would become our family's creed. We have Asperger Syndrome (AS) and, when we are strong and confident, we have what it takes to dare to be different. But when we are not so strong, not so confident, we have one another. We have our family. And on the rare occasion when we are down, dragging our bellies low, we do allow ourselves the freedom to gripe, whine and scream if need be, about just how challenging our lives with AS can be. It is safe for us to scream. Safe, since we have one another to chase the gloom away.

Technically speaking, I realize an Asperger's Syndrome diagnosis only fits the person given it, but realistically, it touches everyone who cares about the one wearing the label. That's why my family decided to write this book together. That is to say, mom would write it and everyone else would offer insight, input, support and, sometimes, a quote or two. This is, after all, a story about how people with special needs in their arms learn to understand and support one another. Perhaps, our world will remind you of yours. All we ask is that as you follow us through our day-to-days, you keep in mind there are no spotlights telling us which direction to go. Instead, we choose to follow a faint flickering glow that always points us toward the place we all go when we need. We call that place home.

Will this book be for everyone on the spectrum? It can be. As with every exploration, the things written in these pages will need to be both pruned and cultivated to fit each individual's situation. I would not have it any other way. To assume or suggest any proposed idea is a one size fits all answer to every prayer is, in my opinion, either exceptionally naive or recklessly presumptuous. We are a group of individuals. We need to be treated as such. How else can we find our own perfect fit?

Liane Holliday Willey, EdD
Michigan
June, 2000

1

Aspie

A house of wonder sits close by.
In this house there are rooms stuffed big with hope and good.
Matters and touchables beyond the extraordinary
call us to be their friends.
Lines do not twist in this house.
Chambers stand straight and certain.
Paths and hallways wind us where we need to go so we are never
lost.
Words spoken are crystal clear.
Visitors park their layers at the door.
We are the architects.
This house is our home.

'She won't speak,' I told my youngest daughter's early childhood teacher. 'She can speak. I know she can. She just won't.'

'Something's not totally right with my daughter. She struggles so when we try to get her dressed or engage her in playtime. Everything has to be her way or no way,' I explained to my few friends.

'Mere seems to have such a good time at school, but she hates being left there in the morning and she is so edgy when it is time to go home. She doesn't want to go and she doesn't want to leave,' I would offer as an excuse to the teachers.

'Why does Mere bite us when she is angry? Why is her anger so incredibly intense?' I would whisper to my husband when no one could hear us.

'Do you notice my daughter isn't playing like the rest of the kids? See her over there, the blonde little girl in the yellow outfit? She is sitting by the other kids, but she is not paying any attention to them. It's like she's in her own world,' I mumbled to the other children's moms who stood next to me behind the pre-school's two-way mirror.

'It's not that her language is delayed, *per se*. She does have some articulation problems, but she seems to be able to echo words I give her. It is just that she does not seem to really understand what certain words mean. She takes everything so literally and will not tolerate it when we say one thing and then do another. That drives her mad!' I said to the doctor.

'How can she be so upset? We are at Disney World for crying aloud. She has been living for Winnie-the-Pooh for four years now. I thought she'd love this stuff!' I thought in my silence.

'I can't put my finger on it, but Mere seems lost. She is doing well in school. She has a friend or two. She has toys she enjoys. She follows the rules and seems very capable of organizing her things and tending to business. In fact, she is the most tenacious kid I know. Once she sets her mind to something, look out! In fact, Lord help those of us who do not follow the rules or do not appreciate the thing she is interested in. But, well…it just does not fit. She's just not like other kids!' I would write in my journal.

'Look at her. Watch her. Don't you see? Something is different. Something's going on. What can it be? What can it be…' I'd say to people I trusted.

These were my mantras. My everyday worries shared with anyone who would listen. These were the answers well meaning teachers, friends and family members gave me:

'She's using selective speech. Don't worry, she'll talk when she's ready.'

'You are the parent. Make her do what you say.'

'Maybe school is just too much for her right now.'

'She bites? Well, you'd better get that under control or she'll be kicked out of school.'

'Oh, she's just fine. She looks like she's playing with the other kids if you ask me.'

'Maybe you just expect too much of her.'

'Maybe she's just too young to enjoy Disney.'

'I do not see it. I just do not. I think you are looking for something to be wrong with your daughter. You must be on some kind of self-fulfilling prophecy here.'

'I'll tell you what's wrong. The child is spoiled. Nothing a good spanking won't cure.'

Six years of doubting, worrying and bickering with those who told me I was exaggerating. Six long years. Finally, Dr. Curt Dyer, a family practice physician and father of an autistic son, suggested we take our daughter to a child development center to determine once and for all if my gut instinct was correct or misled. Dr. Dyer didn't 'see' any solid evidence of a pervasive developmental disorder (PDD), but then again, he knew it was often only the parents of these children who saw the real child. He knew these kids can pretend to be normal in public, that they can copy others' actions well enough to blend into the background. He understood there was a growing body of evidence to suggest there are people on this planet who, on the surface, look completely normal, do well in their school work, find a friend or two to play successfully with, use mostly everyday speech, and yet – suffer somewhere underneath. Dr. Dyer trusted me when I told him my daughter, though obviously bright and capable, was in some way or another off the standard chart.

His belief in my gut gave my husband and me the nudge we needed to take our daughter to Kansas University's Child Development Unit. KU confirmed my instincts were accurate. The terms they used to explain our daughter's behaviors and thoughts matched her far better than the subjective rationales our friends and associates had produced. Gone were statements like '…nothing a good spanking wouldn't cure.' Gone were comments that relied on whimsy and poor judgment. In their place sat real explanations we could lean on for support and valid analyses that picked up our worries and aimed them at the target of help. Old words put into new contexts settled on our ears; words such as approach avoidance, social reasoning, perseverations, theory of mind, rigid thinker, pragmatics, central auditory processing disorder, sensory integration dysfunction, motor dyspraxia, non verbal learning disorder, gaze avoidance and finally – Asperger Syndrome.

Six months later we found the community we belong to. We found others like us. We found out our daughter has Asperger Syndrome.

Now, a test. Asperger's Syndrome (AS) is:

1. a neuro-biological disorder characterized by marked deficiencies in social and communication skills.

2. high-functioning autism.

3. a subclass of non-verbal learning disorders.

4. a pervasive developmental disorder.

5. an excuse for poor behavior.

6. all of the above.

As you may have guessed, AS has been defined as all of the above. No wonder researchers are still in a quandary over determining precisely what AS is, exactly who is affected by it, and most important, what to do about it. The words used to label the diagnosis quite literally depend on where you happen to live in the world, which kind of expert you see and what characteristics the individual affected exhibits. And when I am acerbic, I will add the label depends on what phase the moon is in and how many bones my dog buried that day.

When I attempt to explain AS to those at the beginning of the learning curve, I tend to point them toward the work of Tony Attwood, Ph.D. My own research has shown me his criteria and explanations of AS are the most objective and general in the field to date (see Appendix II for The Australian Scale for Asperger's Syndrome, Garnett & Attwood, 1994). In fact, Attwood's work led me and several members of my family to their own official AS and autism diagnoses. My kin, it seems, is genetically linked to autistic spectrum disorders (ASD).

Two years after my daughter was diagnosed with AS, Dr. Attwood diagnosed me with Residual Asperger's Syndrome in an Adult. It fits. I like it.

Who are we, these aspies, as I call us? We are a mixed group of men and women; boys and girls; tall and short; dark and light; average, smart and super smart people who experience the world in ways just beyond the regular. To us, life is best understood though our intellect rather than our emotional sets, through knowns and givens rather than hypotheticals and maybes. Facts call us. Clear cut answers to pointed questions make sense. Words clothed in too many layers of puns and idioms and euphemisms remain hidden and far from our field of understanding. We prefer sameness and routines to surprises and spur of the moment changes in the day. Though some would say we are rigid thinkers, we would describe ourselves as solid thinkers who are simply certain of our own opinions. Do we have one-track minds? Yes. But those one-track minds are the sort that invent computer chips and rocket ships, divine music and Pulitzer Prize-winning novels. We are tenacious as much as anything else. Are we insensitive to social rules and society's expectations? Do we think things should go by our rules or not go at all? Probably. But we would ask those who strive to follow society's mandates how they came to have the final say in which kinds of rules had to be followed. We would ask them why our aspie way cannot become the given way. Are we blunt and rude? That depends. I suppose we could be on any given day. Just like anyone else, we might slam a door in someone's face, yell at the sales clerk, or hang up on a solicitor. But when we are accused of being blunt and rude because we have provided an honest assessment and straightforward answer to a problem, we sit misaccused and misunderstood.

Tony Attwood and Carol Gray eloquently explain who aspies are quite wonderfully in their article 'The Discovery of "Aspie" Criteria' (*The Morning News*, 1999).[1] Their message: that there is much to savor about aspies, that we are people with two sides. They paint us no longer as people who are stuck crinkled and edgy, but as people bright and shiny-speckled. Attwood and Gray, as true friends of aspies, are 'the glass is half full' people, the true optimists who can really help us grow to our potential. Like Attwood and Gray, I am convinced that if we aspies are met by doom and gloom at every corner we come to, we will certainly wind ourselves around a post until we stand frozen and unable to move. Yes, there is a time for grieving and yes there is a time to wonder what might have been. But if our aspie community is to get to great goals sooner rather than later, we cannot delay that time for too long. As my self-diagnosed aspie father always says, 'Crying will get you nowhere. Off you go.' To where? To centers and counselors and teaches and physicians who can help us find what we need to see. To our families and

---

1   'The Discovery of "Aspie" Criteria', (Fall, 1999) Attwood, T. and Gray, C. *The Morning News*., Volume 11, Number 3.

friends, to our support groups, to our journals. We can see. We just need glasses.

Just as I rely on Attwood's explanations and criteria to make AS tangible, I rely on Carol Gray's work to set it free. Teaching strategies after teaching strategies pour from Gray's endless reservoir of creativity. In uncanny ways, she has the ability to connect with aspies like few others can. Now famous for her Social Story books, she continues to find new ways to teach us how the neurotypical (NT) world turns. Using Attwood and Gray as the major catalysts, our family turned to other researchers in the field who knew how to speak aspie. We studied the work of Simon Baron-Cohen, Uta Frith, Lorna Wing, and Christopher Gillberg. And later, when our minds were as filled with statistics and data as they could get, we turned to the real experts in the AS community. We dove into the autobiographies of aspies, the websites devoted to our world, and the friendships we have established since finding this world. These people are the angels who left their feathers in our nest. Upon their knowledge, we were finally settling in.

In this family, we count among the aspies my father, the self-diagnosed aspie; me, the residual aspie; and my nine-year-old daughter Meredith, the high-functioning aspie. We also include in our warm embrace my mildly autistic little cousin, Kelsey. Moving just beyond our solid circle we wave in our in-betweeners, those among us who carry two or three aspie tricks in their everyday bag. This group includes my thirteen-year-old daughter Lindsey, Meredith's twin sister Jenna and their father and my husband, Tom. Together we are growing up in a family with Asperger's Syndrome.

Certainly, I do not have the definitive answers to all the aspie questions. If only I did. What I do have is my own story, my own blueprint. And so came this book. It is my hope the book will allow the neurotypical world to see the sights as we adult aspies often do. It is my intention to explore and illuminate those circumstances and situations that tug at our aspie minds and hearts.

And most important, it is my wish to share the comforter I managed to knit together from all the bits and pieces of insight and understanding I've collected from everywhere and everyone who has influenced me and mine, so that others will be made warmer from having shared some time with my thoughts.

2

Too Close to the Maddening Crowd

Imagine for a moment. Close your eyes. Pretend. You are an aspie. Think. You see faces, they scrunch up and move about, their features swimming in circles. If they send you a message, you do not receive it. Picture yourself in a lunchroom, a party, the mall, a crowded hallway. Watch the walls of these rooms, note the ceilings, look at the floor. Soon, these lines and angles will appear to touch, leaving you trapped in the small space your body is left with. Hold on tightly, for soon this little spot will start to spin you and twirl you and snap you in half. Listen carefully. You'll have to learn the hard way that there is more than one message behind strings of words. Expect to look stupid and ignorant and ridiculous until you learn that message. Get used to being teased and laughed at, ignored and left-out, until you learn how to play the game – the 'normal' game. You know, it's the game where certain rules and expectations about how people should look, sound, behave and even think, are passed down to the neurotypicals but not to you. Know that you won't go crazy over this, though there will be times when you come to doubt your sanity. You'll worry. As you should, for unless you are willing to look, listen and learn everything you can about the neurotypicals, you will be trapped in their maze. But you will not give up. You will fight to salvage what is yours – your heart, your soul, your morals, your ethics, your loves and your needs. And then, when you are comfortable in your own skin, you will then do what needs to be done to join the neurotypicals in their game. You know you may never beat them at their game, but you give a little smile in the hopes that you will at least learn how to play without getting your butt kicked.

I met him at a monster sized, retail warehouse. It was a cavernous building with concrete floors and an exposed skeleton of the building's framework. The noise was so piercing and sharp it sounded like we were in a bucket of tin. He was standing between two aisles filled with books and computer software. My favorite aisle. I noticed him immediately. He wasn't looking at the books or the software. He looked to be looking for a friend. Or at least someone to pretend they were his friend. I figured that all the people hurrying by him without so much as a nod or a hello were uninterested in being that friend. Maybe they thought they were just too busy.

I never heard his name. He didn't tell me that. But he did tell me a whole lot more.

'I know lots of foreign languages,' he said as a way of introducing himself to me.

'You do?' I asked, impressed as I always am by people who have an ear for languages.

'Yes. I know French, Italian, German, Spanish and Latin. Latin is a dead language. You can't use it in conversation, you know. But I like it anyway. My parents taught me all those languages. Well, they made sure I learned them, anyway. They taught me some of them and I taught myself the others. Latin is my favorite. Do you know any foreign languages?'

'Believe it or not, I do know Latin. That is, I used to. I studied it in school and I also know some Spanish. I wish I knew Italian and French, but I don't think I could speak German. The accent is so difficult.'

'Latin is a good language. It's the basis of our English, you know. Mostly that is. Spanish is nice, too. It's a whole lot like Italian. Why don't you study them now?'

'I should, shouldn't I? I guess because I'm too busy with my kids and my job to take the time off to study. But, maybe one day I will! Thanks for giving me the idea.'

'I don't have kids. I like kids. I just don't have any. I live with my parents. I don't have to, I mean I could live alone if I wanted to, but I like being with my parents and I don't mind living with them. They're getting old now and I help them around the house and things,' he offered with an expression that told me he wasn't lying or trying to make any excuses.

'Are your parents here now?'

'No, I'm just out shopping by myself.'

'But you don't have a shopping cart. How are you going to carry all of your things?' I asked, always looking for answers to the obvious.

'Oh. I. Well. You see. Are you going to teach your kids any languages? You should, you know. How old are they? Because if they are young, they will pick them up quickly. I was little when my parents had me learn languages. My dad is an engineer and my mom is a teacher. They had lots of time for me. We lived all over the place. My dad was transferred a lot. I didn't get to go out of the country, so I couldn't really use all my languages. But I did get to speak Spanish when we went to California. My mom stayed home with me. She's very nice, my mom is. Both of my parents are. They are great!'

I began to wonder just how much shopping my new friend was going to do. It seemed to me that he was stuck in first gear, unable to face the highway this store laid out for its customers. I only shopped the store because I am rather addicted to bargain hunting and this store had plenty of bargains. In other words I was motivated to shop there. Very motivated. If I wasn't, I would not have walked beyond the front door. Too many noises, too many visual distractions, too many bits and pieces of this and that floating around here and there to attack the calm. By the look of things, I guessed my friend felt the atmosphere was as tingly as I did.

'Do you like shopping here,' I asked, testing my theory.

'I. Hmm… It's…they sell a lot of interesting things. Do you like shopping here?'

'No. I don't. I come here because I like to find bargains and because this store is so easy for me to find my way around. I like the symmetry of the place. But it is far too noisy and far too busy for my personal tastes. If I didn't really like cheap stuff, I wouldn't be here.'

'Me neither. When we lived in California, I…' I sat back against a stack of books and listened to more of my friend's stories. My friend seemed relieved to have found a kindred spirit. I was, too.

My family came by us a few times to see if I was all right or lost or interested in following them around the store. I nodded I was OK when they strolled by us. My husband knew what was going on. He was well used to me finding the lonely souls that struggle through shopping malls, libraries, book stores…the world within the world. Once he knew I was OK and not about to be kidnapped or harmed in any way, he scooted past us to return to his shopping. Two of my girls followed their dad, leaving me a questioning glance but nothing more audible than a, 'Hi Mom. Bye Mom.' My aspie daughter left her father and came to my side.

'Who's he,' she whispered in my ear.

'He's a new friend I just met,' I whispered back.

She stared at him. She and I are both stare people. We look at people as if they were statues in a museum. Sometimes my daughter will even touch the people, if they are standing quite still. Then, when the person wakes from the shock of the touch, my daughter will come running to me with her hand over her mouth and her eyes as big as saucers. 'Mom,' she'll say. 'I thought that person was a statue and so I touched them and they weren't and they looked at me and I am so embarrassed.' 'Oh well,' I'll answer. 'I'm sure they aren't mad at you. You probably just startled them.'

'Is this your daughter?' my friend asked.

'Yes, it is. This is my youngest girl. She has two sisters running around here with their dad.'

'Hi.'

'Honey, say hi to my friend.'

'Hi.'

'How are you?'

'Good.'

'That's nice. Do you know any foreign languages? I do. I know...'

My daughter was mesmerized by the man. She stared and stared and stared, but never said a word. Our friend told us all about his childhood, how his mom and he would read books about other countries and go to museums, and how his dad and he would work on model airplanes and practice their Latin together. He really seemed like a happy man. He was funny and bright and very articulate. It didn't bother me one bit that he spoke only of foreign languages and his childhood. It was interesting to hear about the history of different languages, the ways in which they are alike and different. I enjoyed picturing him as a happy little guy with his mom and dad and I silently thanked the Heavens that he didn't have to spend his young years alone and sad in the corner of his room. I would have bet he didn't have many friends his own age to play with. Maybe it was a good thing, after all, that he moved around so much. It didn't give him much time to be hurt by his peers. Kids like the kind he must have been usually are.

After a good long time, my husband and the other girls came to collect my aspie and me. They exchanged brief hellos to our friend and explained we needed to get back home to let our dogs out of the house. Our friend told us he liked dogs and that he hoped they were all right. We smiled and assured him they were no doubt fine and then left him standing where he was an hour ago. The spot he hadn't left since I first found him.

When we were about to leave the building, I turned and saw my friend one last time. He was trying to make eye contact with the people looking at books. He would smile, and kind of dip his head below theirs, trying to find their eyes – trying to make a friend. Why wasn't I surprised to see no one was looking at him? Why didn't it shock me to see their heads remained lowered and their gazes protected from his? Too bad for them, I thought as I turned to walk away, they missed a great opportunity to meet a very interesting nice man. An aspie, no doubt.

What is it about us aspies that makes other kinds of people itchy? Do we smell badly? While I will admit there are some in our club who find hygiene to be a nebulous concept at best, most of my aspie friends smell fresh and clean and, I might add, they never smell like some NTs I know who seem to have rocked and rolled in a field of overly-ripe and wetly-weeping gardenias. If it is not our smell, is it something about the way we look? True, some of us are sloppy dressers totally unaware of fashion musts and clothes laws, but so are plenty of NTs. Comedian Ellen de Generes once said fashion designers make the clothes they do to try and see what they can get away with. Seems to me, she's right. And it isn't us aspies who are wearing those experiments.

If not our smell or personal style, is it the disregard some aspies have for personal space issues that keep NTs a bit suspicious of our character? If so, I can relate to that. I am of the opinion that far away is better than near and close. I am unnerved when people come into my arena and happy when they are far enough from me to cause me to put on my glasses if I want to see them sharply. But I am not the lone aspie on this wave length. Loads of other aspies agree with me, they too becoming quickly annoyed when anyone puts nothing but a few inches between themselves and our person. Still, if the personal space issue is the issue that keeps the NTs at bay, I wonder why they don't simply try to find a something to put between themselves and the aspie, say a table or a chair. It strikes my mind as easy to alter the personal space problem. So, I think, it must not be that. Perhaps it is the aspie's tendency to go on and on and on about a topic. Maybe our keen interest in the details of our favorite obsession bore or overwhelm those around us. Could be...but then again, I've been in the company of countless NTs who must assume I am enthusiastically interested in hearing about their boss's oddities, their spouse's failings, their neighbor's shocking behaviors or their trips to places I would never visit. Don't we all sooner or later talk about stuff others find boring and tedious? I have hunches NTs turn from aspies because there is something about our demeanor that wrinkles their smooth. Admittedly, aspies often sway, tic, and look far off or stare intently. We might mutter under our breath, or talk all over other people's talking, or monologue, or walk away from a conversation before it was meant to be finished. Yes, those must seem annoying to most anyone around us, but are they reason enough to avoid us forever and a day? In the whole scheme of life, aren't those merely tweaks from normal social channels and not gross deviations from acceptable?

I start to wonder if NTs turn from aspies because of something I will never be able to see or touch. Is there, I wonder, some something that wells up deep inside of the NT belly, some instinctual mandate, that keeps NTs away from our aspie island? Or am I reading too much into all of this? Could it be that it is just too much work to try and figure out those who strike us as too different or too weird? For my part, anyway, I know few things make me happier than the moments I discover another aspie in our midst. And I think the attitude is mutual. Nothing lights up the aspie face like the realization they are spending time with a fellow thinker. How cool it is to be able to finally, at long last, say things like, 'Me too!' and 'Yes! That's it exactly.' How awesome it is to see other human beings plug their ears when the noise creeps in, or pull in their bodies tight and small when the maddening crowds get too near, or flap their hands when the anxiety mounts too strong a charge. Few things make me feel as confident and serene as the presence of other aspies. I cannot, therefore, blame NTs if they choose to be around their own kind more often than not. But I can look down on them with hurt and sadness in my eyes when I see them running and hiding from us. And I can look at them with anger and dislike when they shun and ridicule the aspie. That act is an unforgivable.

I think about my daughter and her future. I don't want her to get tangled-up in this world. I want things to be easier for her. I want the world to work harder when it meets people who are different. I think of older aspies. I worry about their quality of living. Their caregivers probably find them nuts. But of course, they aren't. They are caught in their aspieness, they are caught in what they know. What they don't know is how to teach others who they are, what they require and what they could surely do without. My daughter, the older aspies – they no doubt appear to NTs as bumps which should be avoided. Shame on them. I see aspies as books with unusual plots, multi-layered characters and far-out settings. I sit and shake my head in disbelief when I meet up with NTs who aren't interested in turning our pages. If only they knew...if only they knew what they were missing.

Consider the stories we aspies can tell. We can describe a situation like no one else. We can tell you what intangibles feel like and secret flavors taste like. We can describe for you, in unbelievable depth, the intricate details of our favorite obsessions. Think how grand that would be if you shared that obsession. We can teach you how important it is to follow your instincts, for many of us have very strong gut knowledge, sort of like the way many blind folks have excellent hearing. You know, one gift for another. We can teach you new meanings for new words, because we like to make up words that strike us as rich and important and to the point, even if they aren't in any dictionary. It's part of our pragmatic nature. And we can teach you to follow the right path instead of the wrong, for few on this planet have a moral code as stringent as ours. When our big people tell us it is wrong to steal and cheat and lie, we listen and listen well. Even when NTs tell us we are tattling or being too literal or missing the point of your theories, we persevere and do what is right. We have to. We are rule followers and rule enforcers who can help others to see how much better the world would run if everyone obeyed the letter of the law. Just think, there would be no more car accidents because someone ran a red light or drove too fast; there would be room for everyone's luggage on the airplane; no one would ever sit in your designated seat again; you would always keep your place in line; you would get ahead in this world, even if you didn't know anyone in power; you could believe what you heard; you could sleep with a clear conscience.

Together…together we can do so much. If it were within my reach, I would ask the NTs to meet us half way. I would ask them to let us teach them what we know in exchange for what they know. For example, it seems to me NTs seem to experience more time with peace and serenity than I do. They can leisurely bask in the sun while I obsessively follow the weather patterns to see just how long that sun will last. They go to a party knowing they'll enjoy time with a friend they haven't seen in some time, while I lament going to the party for fear there will be no one there as interested in the flow patterns of the furniture arrangement as I am. NTs can look forward to a new job with hope and optimism and tummy tickling enthusiasm while I cringe and shake at the thought of new faces, strange routines, and exhausting mind twists. NTs know from the get-go which line in which office one should stand in for which set of problems and concerns while I stand there in a daze trying not to look suspicious under the 'anyone looking suspicious will be arrested' signs. Normies know what to do when company comes to stay for an hour or even a week, whereas I fidget and fumble with the fear that I'll surely serve the wrong kind of coffee, or lay out the wrong kinds of towels, or change the conversation topics too quickly, or complain too loudly about the smells my guests brought with them, or misinterpret the words everyone else nods and smiles at, or talk over the it's-time-to-go signs the NT will eventually send me, or leave the room before the conversation has found a natural end. In short, I fear I'll mess everything up until no one wants to visit me again. 'Just be yourself,' friends will tell me. 'Just do what comes naturally,' they say. Such words sound believable only to those who have never been laughed at for their silly mistakes or shamed for trying too hard to please.

I am envious of the fact that so much in this life comes as givens to the NTs. I grow weary just thinking about all the things I will mess up, and I get jealous when it comes to me that the solutions to these tricks are passed on to NTs in non-verbal, yet substantial ways the average normie learns without even realizing they have learned it. I want things to be as easy for aspies as they are for NTs. I am embarrassed that these seemingly easy sorts of things are the very things that make me blink, stop and stare at my feet. In the end, I feel reduced to nothingness and confused to oblivion for missing so much. I feel incomplete. In the echo of the scream, 'How do you know all that?' I think about giving up.

The reality of life tells me that aspies need to unlock the mainstay mysteries, if we hope to go beyond the surface in our understanding of NT life. Lucky for me, I have always been intrigued by the mainstream. My own father taught me years ago to watch, learn, listen and memorize. And so I do. With super sleuth tenacity, virtually anyone can learn how to figure out at least some of the stuff that goes with normie life. Using mental imaging as a virtual diary, I write what I experience – what I see, hear, feel and even smell – on my memory cards, which I then categorize and store in areas I imagine to be neat boxes kept in a giant room of my brain. When in need I can go to that 'room' and unlock the drawer that has the information I need to review before I enter the realm of the NT. Slowly, because so many years have walked by me at this point in my life, I find I need to visit that room less and less, but I gain great comfort in knowing my research is with me should I need to grab it before my nervous tension grabs me and leaves me for gone.

On some days, I am not able to visualize this imaginary diary and storage system. On those days I try to jump-start my collective lessons learned by literally recording what I am experiencing and all the problems I'm facing as I wander about. There is something sound and straight about writing my problems and my concerns smack down on a clean sheet of paper. When I write or even draw an image of my confusion, I am more likely than not to tap into the part of my mind that holds a similar set of situations I have already lived through to tell about. Writing and drawing things helps me to access my memory banks and more. When my issues are visually laid out before me, I can usually find a way to apply logic and intelligence to the situation. It's as if the problem, once put on paper, stands as something I can be objective about and therefore somewhat removed from, so that I am then able to look at the situation without the layers of frustration and hurt attached to it. Once a safe distance away, I can slowly begin a process of self-questioning. I can slowly solve the mystery.

I truly believe social understanding is only possible if the aspie is comfortable with the notion of self-questioning and at the same time, leery of self-doubt. When I was growing up and facing too many of my own self-doubts, the very kind that served to keep me from self-analysis, my father used to say to me, 'What is the worst that can happen? Will you die? No? Then do not worry about it so much.' This deceptively simple line of reasoning has come to my rescue for decades now. Any time I stop in the middle of my tracks, I ask myself, 'What is the worst that can happen to me if I continue in what I am doing?' Unless I picture my dead body in a coffin, I forge ahead and do what I need to do to think my way across the tracks and into the pretty field.

This is all about the aspie needing to know it is safe to face our confusion. The biggest problem for me is in figuring out which of life's moments cause me the greatest amounts of confusion. I use visualization to help me with this problem, too. I begin the process by picturing myself wandering through a typical day. I imagine myself experiencing the kinds of situations I will likely face. In some of these images, I see myself confidently moving about, fully aware of what I need to do and which way I need to go. These are the images I begin with first. They provide me with a bit of security. For example, I am perfectly safe when I see myself getting my children up from their sleep, making them breakfast, sending them on to their school. I am fine thinking about the work I need to do on my latest projects, the parts of the house that need cleaning, the dinner I will make that night. These images put me on a ride that is so gentle I do not even need a belt to buckle me in.

The images that follow however, switch the ride into high gear. Suddenly, I need not only a belt, but also an air bag and a safety cage. These images run the gauntlet. I see myself struggling to pick the behaviors I need to coast through a gathering of my husband's business associates. I see myself becoming a bundle of nerves as I try to figure out exactly how to take money out of my savings account, or how to mail a package overseas, or how to find a store on an unfamiliar side of my town. I picture myself running conversations in my mind with this meaning attached to this word and then that meaning attached to that word, over and over and over again until loads of meanings have found their way to loads of the words being spoken to me, all this to be as sure as I can that I'm not overlooking any tiny speech nuances that will make it impossible for me to know for certain I am accurately figuring out what is being said to me. It doesn't take long to feel as if I'm turning upside down and I worry, if I can topple, what must my aspie daughter be feeling like. I picture my daughter. Are her nerves pinched when she goes to birthday parties even though she wants to be there? Does ordering food in a restaurant upset her because she has no idea what the food will really look like and taste like? Does she know how to order a movie ticket and buy popcorn at the theater, or do the movie timetables and schedules and treat choices jumble her up? Is she comfortable telling people when she is confused, or is she more likely to keep it all inside until everything festers into a big messy sore? Does she beat herself up when she misses the point?

These tasks, seemingly more of the simplistic, really are not. Each depends on smooth joints and a smooth chain of events. I tell my daughter to think of life's experiences as sets of procedures she can follow the moment she finds a good map and an understandable set of directions. I teach her that once she has identified the things that confuse her, she can begin to map out a way through them. My daughter is learning how to do this, but she often needs help in discerning which details are important and which are superfluous. For example, when we ask her to take notes on people in general, we find she typically records what they are wearing, what their jewelry looks like, what color their hair is and so forth. We encourage her to write those things down, for they are important to her, but we also prompt her to write down exactly what it is about these people and what they are doing that confuses her. We teach her to video record them in her own mind so that she can replay the sequence of events over and over until she begins to find a pattern or until we can help her figure one out. One by one, we work with our daughter through her confusing moments. One by one, we direct her attention, direct her thoughts, and direct her analysis until she has memorized the kinds of scenarios she will encounter as she goes about her life. Direct instruction from self-analysis that is protected from self-doubt. That's what works for us. Most of the time...

Aspies find it hard to generalize from one situation to another. Anything the least bit novel about what we're doing, and we look at it as if it were the first time we had ever had the experience. One situation is not like the next, in our minds, unless they are identical in virtually every aspect. For instance, despite the fact that I have been traveling rather extensively since I was a teenager, I am still largely unable to successfully navigate my way through the situations that surround traveling. Each and every time I travel, I face a certain disaster of one sort or another. I have sat for hours under the sign that says, 'Your hotel van will pick you up here' precisely waiting for the van to show, until a kind stranger somehow noting my ignorance, told me I needed to call the hotel to tell them I was waiting 'here'. I have made my way to hotels I thought were mine until the hotel manager finally found a way to convince me I was not on the register and had to have made a mistake. I have gotten lost for hours on end in two-street towns that are home to no more than a thousand people. I have left airports in a froth of fury, so upset has it made me to see so many rules broken…luggage brought on the plane that is far bigger than the regulation size, people trying to sit in my seat by using the excuse 'they're all the same you know', individuals jumping ahead of others in line, people hogging my arm rest, tray tables left down when we are landing, crowds rushing to get off even though the plane has not come to a complete and final stop…bother, I get sticky just thinking about those bad behaviors. But the point is this, the least bit of change in a routine or an experience can be all the change it takes to confuse the aspie.

Knowing confusion will be my middle name for a long time to come, I have decided to do something that helps me through the problems it causes, rather than continually trying to end the confusion. I cannot decide if this is a good idea or a bad one, but for now, it comes to me as the only idea I can get my arms around. The moment I recognize confusion coming my way, I reach in my comfort kit and will myself to chill-out. My purse holds my comfort kit. It is typically stuffed with ear plugs I can use to shut out the chaos, a small cotton bag of eucalyptus smelling salts I turn to when other smells gag, a squishy ball I can set my jitters on, a bendable wire toy I can concentrate on when my focus wanders too far, a pad of paper I can put my thoughts and worries and questions on, my favorite pen that puts thin ink on the paper just like I like it, big sticks of bubble gum to occupy my mouth when I sense my words are running amuck, a spritz bottle of mineral water I use to cool my hot face, and my current read which will transfer me to a place far from one that might be unsettling me. Nothing so out of the ordinary. Everything so essential to me. My calm tools. My emergency kit. I think everyone should have one.

The fact is, when our anxieties are kept low, our efforts to concentrate on the world are sharpened. This makes me wonder why schools insist their students come to class without any of their home comforts. Doesn't that seem oddly restrictive? We allow toddlers to carry a blanket or a stuffed bunny, but a handful of months later we insist they put all their comforts into a box and face the real world unprotected and detached. It is a wonder any child can leave the comfort of their room. Think how the aspie must feel. Think how much safer they would feel if they could bring specials from home to school. Thankfully, our school system allows its students to do just that. My aspie daughter and her almost aspie twin bring seat cushions to sit on. The aspie girl brings her key chain collection and her extensive collection of folders, pens, journals and organizers. Every child is encouraged to bring stims and earphones and ear plugs and stuff that makes their day lighter to carry. It strikes me as sad and wrong that our school is more the exception than the rule. Now carry on the thought to the business world. Can employees decorate their space as they need? Can they find comfort from wearing a big set of chunky ear phones necessary for them to keep out the noise so they can hear their own thoughts? Are they allowed to chomp on big wads of gum in a corporate meeting? Are they encouraged to wear their favorite pair of pants every day or are they expected to follow an NT dress code? We all know what the answer so often is, but can anyone explain it so that it makes any real sense?

Self-help eventually becomes the primary goal. It is also a way of life, a pattern aspies must come to trust and rely on. It is a manner of being that should be as comfortable as a favorite pair of slippers and as comforting as a bar of luscious chocolate. Aspies might need to work harder to understand and accommodate their needs, but they can do it. Eventually, if she really wants to, the aspie will learn how to fit in more often than she falls out.

Fitting in. What a very relative term. As I spend more and more time talking to more and more aspies from all over the spectrum, I discover we all have our own thoughts on just how important it is to fit in. Some of us have no desire to walk the NT walk. Some of us are very intent on becoming more NT than aspie. Still others of us are happy to play NT and live aspie. The point that sticks for me is the idea that everyone deserves the right to interact with others in their own way. I will never judge if it is wrong to pretend or better to admit your differences out loud. How could I? How could anyone? Still, I find myself relying on the belief that when the need shakes us, we aspies can train ourselves to help our NT supporters by trying as hard as we can to put our aspieness on hold. On hold. Not out to pasture. For a few minutes, if not an hour or a whole day, we can likely learn to pretend we fit in. Do I like to pretend? Not particularly. Do I do it? Often. The effort it takes to pretend often costs me less than does the stress of NT/AS communication gaffes.

PLAYING PRETEND (EVERY ONCE IN A WHILE)

○ Echo others. Laugh when they do, frown when they do, nod when they do. But take care not to echo so well you appear to be mocking others. If someone laughs loud, you might choose to laugh softly. If you see someone nodding with their whole body language, you might simply nod your head once. In other words, echo, but modify.

○ Go prepared. Before you attend an event, study topics you are likely to discuss and situations you are likely to experience. For instance, if you are going to an art gallery with your wife's business associates, learn what kinds of displays and exhibits they will show so you can study them in advance. Then plan a few things you can say about some of those things. Remember not to monopolize the conversation, but do plan on speaking a few intelligent sentences about this or that item of interest.

○ Ask for help. Ask someone you trust with NT ways to help you find your way through the event you are attending. It might be an event as common as a parent/teacher conference or one as unique as an antique auction. Ask the friend what you should wear, what you should expect to have happen, the roles the people there might play, and what kinds of manners – casual, serious, sophisticated or relaxed – you should try to emulate.

○ Create a few personae you can put on like you put on a coat. Consider yourself an actor who is able to become someone else for the benefit of the play. My favorite role is the comedic role. I like telling jokes and making people laugh. I also like playing the academic. It is easy for me to express my knowledge on subjects I have studied beforehand. Put another way, I try to mask my nervous tension by joking. I try to hide my worries by stating facts and obscure information. Find a persona you can rely on when you are too nervous to be yourself. But never forget that even the persona is you…just a different you.

The maddening crowd can come after us aspies. It can bite our heels, nip our fingers and tweak our toes. It can trip us, shove us and bury us alive. If we let it. With the help of our own conscious discoveries, our support teams, our sense of self-confidence and self-appreciation, and our honest and energetic tenacity, I truly believe those of us who belong to the aspie community can learn how to tame even the biggest beasts in the jungle. Maybe we will never reach out and pet them, maybe they will never curl up at our feet and purr, but with a strong will and a direct focus, we can learn how to keep them from eating us up for supper. And if the NTs are very lucky, we will invite them over for dessert.

3

Holding on to What Makes Sense

Close your eyes to all that lights.
Make your ears to turn away.
Bundle tight your voice.
Keep things known within your quiet.
Share not the time you moved within.
Tell nothing found about.
The world was meant for guessing games
and opinions play keep away.

'Fat grandmothers don't ride bikes.'

'Did you hear what she just said?' my grandmother demanded of my mom.

'Yes, I heard. Liane, let your grandmother ride your new bike,' came her reply.

'No. She is too fat and she will break it.'

'You shouldn't talk to your grandmother like that,' the grandmother replied, as angry as a wet hen.

And off I rode, on my bike, no fat grandmas with me. *Gosh*, I clearly remember thinking, *why is everyone so mad at me? What did I do this time?* The adult me can now look back and tell the eight-year-old me, I had hurt my grandmother's feelings. The adult me now knows there are some adages that are good only in theory. When I was eight, I had no way of knowing the world was indeed fibbing when it told me: the truth cannot hurt you, honesty is the best policy, the truth will set you free, omitting information is the same thing as lying, and so on and so forth. Thankfully, my parents bucked the real world and stayed true to each of those sentiments. It gave me a tremendous amount of comfort to know that, at least in our home, the truth was all of those things it was reported to be. Their support of my sticking to the truth, no matter what, was in many ways one of the most important things they could have done for me. From that platform, I could later, much later, learn how to play the regular world's truth-bending game.

I did not easily stumble my way into the knowledge that there is a socially acceptable manner of truth telling. In fact, if I am pushed, I will tell I have yet to prove my understanding is completely reliable. It seems I will go to my grave mystified by a world that thinks it fine to talk about sex and drugs and violence on the open movie screen or in children's classrooms, but wrong to tell what dress size Aunt Lucy wears or how much money the neighbor makes. Likewise, I will never understand why people from the regular world are so aghast when the truth from the obvious comes at them. For example, could it really have been a shock when my aspie daughter exclaimed to a waiter, 'You should wash your hands after you touch people's money'. Surely the waiter knows money is filthy and food is clean. Surely this comment from my daughter is not nearly as offensive as the waiter's dirty hands on our lunch. Why then, are we aspies in the minority when it comes to saying it like it is?

'Why,' my aspie will ask, 'do people get mad when I tell the truth?' What a difficult question to answer. We begin by trying to teach her the regular world has its own set of rules that will, when it really comes to it, take complete precedence over any maxim including all those which underscore the importance of truth. Basically, we tell her, there are times for full disclosure and times for keeping things hush-hush. I try to explain to her that it is perfectly acceptable and indeed expected for her to tell her parents everything and anything, painful, embarrassing, rude, or otherwise. I find that when she tells us *everything*, we can then take the opportunity to help her analyze which of those things are best to be kept from the public's ears and which of those things it is best to share. I confess we are all still struggling with this issue, but to date we have decided on the following rules:

- o When in doubt, think it, but don't say it.

- o If you don't have anything nice to say to someone, do not say anything at all.

- o Write in your journal when something really bothers you, rather than exclaiming it to the world. Then bring your journal home and let Mom and Dad help you figure out what to do with the thought.

Of course we run a great risk when we help our aspie to realize the complete truth is something we occasionally need to hide a bit. This leads her straight into the fear that people are not telling her the truth and the truth is all she readily understands and all she wants to hear. I know this fear well. It turns the world into a wobbly place, a place that moves faster than the eye, a place that hides behind too many masks. How can we learn to trust if we are forever questioning the validity and reliability of those around us? How can we learn to become confident people, if we think our accomplishments and our best efforts will be mauled by half truths and no truths?

Imagine how it feels to think like an aspie…we have learned to worry: Is my school project truly a wonderful project or was the teacher just trying to make me feel good? Do you really want to be my friend or are you just coming to my house to play with my toys? Does this outfit really make me look attractive or is my date too embarrassed to tell me it makes me look like a clown? Is this car really a solid car or is the salesman just trying to make a sale? If you were to ask us, we would say it is far better to live in reality than in deception. We would tell you we are most likely going to miss the body language and eye gazes and vocal tics that indicate to NTs something is not totally true about a situation. We would tell you it is right to tell the truth and wrong to lie. If you were to ask us, we would say the truth is the only thing that makes sense.

However, even I will acknowledge there can be very valid reasons for keeping certain things quiet. For instance, if the truth will hurt someone for no good reason and if nothing good or valuable will come from hearing the truth, then even I would acknowledge there is no logical or sound reason for telling it. As an example: What good did it do when I told a friend there was no way her daughter could compete against mine on the athletic field because my child had a superior set of physical genes? Believe it or not, when I said this I really did think I was helping the person out, helping her to see she should be realistic about her child's finish in a race because when objectively analyzed, it was my daughter who had the perfect bone structure for the sport, as well as the innate talent it took to succeed. I really did think objectivity would make the other mother smile and applaud her daughter for her effort alone, so that she would not feel so beat-up by the girl's loss. It never dawned on me my version of the truth, no matter how real it might have been, would cause the mother pain. Of course, it did. I now know that I wasn't the one to help this mother come to realistic expectations for her daughter. Someone else, a caring coach or a trusted relative, would have been the person to do so, if in fact anyone should have.

I have had to climb on top of the mountain of my mistakes to see that sometimes the truth costs more than it is worth. I now readily admit the NT world is on to something when they keep quiet the truths that cannot really make any improvement on someone's life. That idea, even I can go along with. It is the very gist of the truth idea we now try to pass on to our aspie girl.

While I am finally able to put a lid on my desire to tell others certain kinds of truths, I have yet to learn how to keep myself from telling too much about myself. Self-disclosure of the most candid kind is a true aspie trademark and it is apparently one I wear big and boldly. I have to say I do not know why it is so difficult for others to accept what I have to say about myself, but I am learning this is a notion I do not have to understand. It is simply a notion I need to acknowledge and then respect. I am told by my NT friends and my mostly NT children this self-disclosure habit of mine is a most embarrassing habit. I cannot count on all my fingers and all my toes how many times my children have yanked me down to whisper loudly in my ear, 'Mom! You aren't supposed to tell people THAT!!' Nor can I keep track of how many times my husband has given me the 'Don't go there' nod. I have gathered that their reticence to let me tell all has something to do with the 'time and place' theory. The one that states, 'There is a time and place for everything. Now is neither the time nor the place.' What the kids and their father and my friends have yet to help me discover with one hundred per cent accuracy is, when is the time and where is the place?

Apparently there is a strong notion among NTs that certain subjects are taboo for general consumption and best reserved for specific counsels. For example, virtually anything having to do with the physical body has to be saved for physicians' ears only, unless of course, we're talking about athletic prowess. Those kinds of talks can be openly shared. Unless one starts to brag or boast, in which case the audience is likely to think negative thoughts about the speaker, the 'Isn't she stuck-up?' kinds of thoughts. Similarly, anything unpleasant having to do with my marriage has to be kept private, unless I'm among a group of women (never men; men can talk to men and women to women, the two cannot mix) who are bent on discussing their husbands' failures as a spouse, provider or father. Then, it's okay to complain about my man and our relationship; however, and this is a big however, I need to go slowly if I am going to attempt to tell good things about my guy. I'm told that too many good stories about my man would make other women jealous of my situation and thus angry toward me for having something they do not have themselves. Ifs, buts, howevers, not nows, in that case, not in this case…who can figure this mess out? The NT custom of accepted and unaccepted self-disclosure is frankly one I am not likely to master. Not in the foreseeable future, anyway.

Luckily for her, my aspie daughter is not a self-discloser. She is the kind of aspie who wants to fit in and be accepted just like everyone else. Unlike her mom, she is not happy leaning towards detachment. It causes her no end of worry and trauma when she notes she is the least bit different from her peers. I wish this were not so, but I can only wish. No matter how hard my husband and I try to teach her it is admirable to be happy in her own skin, she tries often to wear someone else's. Her ability to echo others is uncanny. She is exceptionally good at inventing herself according to the model someone else has put before her. She copies everything from vocal tones and inflections, to manners of dress and behavior, to patterns of logic and reasoning. She's like a chameleon, this one is. On one hand this pleases us, for it is a very crafty way to fit in. It means she can, if she so chooses, 'pretend to be normal' just like her mom does. On the other hand, the scary hand, our daughter's propensity to follow blindly the way of her peers leaves her an exposed child, a very impressionable and very easy to influence young girl. This reality sends my husband and I to sleep with our eyes wide open for we know too well our daughter is ripe and ready for the bad man's picking.

We live with the fear that someday someone will harm our aspie. We know, as any aspie family knows, that far too many aspies have been lured into dangerous situations, talked into doing others or themselves harm, and led into the illegal by way of false words wrapped up in pretty packages. Yes, there are few more ethical and rule-abiding than the aspie, but ours are the children that can be convinced of things by smooth talkers, so accustomed are they to taking words at their literal level. Ours are the kids that believe what they hear, so unfamiliar are they with the reasons and the signs behind lying and deception. They are the innocents in the audience who do not think to look under the table to see if the magician's rabbits are nesting there; they actually believe the rabbits do live in the big black hat. We need to teach them there are bad people in the world who will do bad things to them, if they are not very careful. Yes, we run the risk of turning them into paranoid adults, but it is a risk we have to take. I hope we can train them to listen, watch and learn through less trusting and honest eyes. I hope we can teach them to think more NT when it comes to their own safety. Until that day comes, we have had to directly instruct our aspie and even her mostly NT sisters that there are certain things they cannot ever be led to take part in. We discuss and then play out scenarios that would come from the list. We do this often for we believe it can make the difference between safety and fatal harm.

THE BEWARE LIST

o Never do anything illegal. Stealing is illegal. Borrowing without permission is illegal. Going through someone's home or things, without permission, is illegal. Entering a store before it is open for the public is illegal. Going into a theater or any kind of performance where tickets are sold, without buying a ticket, is illegal. Signing someone's name other than your own to any piece of official paperwork such as a contract, a check, a credit card, or a report card, is illegal.

o Never go anywhere with anyone, not a friend or relative, unless your parents give you their permission on that very day to go with the person or unless the person trying to take you somewhere knows your family's secret code word. The secret code word is a

word you and your family say when an emergency has
happened that made your parents call someone else to
pick you up or take you somewhere. When you hear
the secret word, it means your parents gave the person
who said it permission to come get you and take you
where you need to go.

o Never, ever go anywhere with a stranger unless he or
she knows the secret code word. Strangers will lie to
you to get you to come with them. They might tell you
they are sick or that they need your help or that your
parents sent them to get you. Unless they know the
secret word, you have to assume they are lying to you.

o If someone tries to get you to do something you have
been taught not to do, get away from them as fast as
you can. Run and scream, if they are scaring you. Tell
your parents, or someone your parents have told you
that you can trust, what has happened.

o Learn to trust your instincts. If you feel something is
not right, if you are suddenly frightened or upset in any
way by anything, leave the situation and tell someone
you trust about it. Do not stay or put up with anything
that upsets your emotions.

o Never talk about private matters in public. Private
matters include: personal hygiene, body parts that are
covered up by underwear, academic and learning
problems, your siblings' diaries, your parents'
arguments, family disagreements.

Of course, the 'Beware' list is the kind of list every parent shares
with every young child. As it happens, the aspie will most likely
need this kind of instruction even when their chronological
years are well ahead of the typical NT's young and innocent
years. This is not because aspies are incapable or slow thinkers,
we just stay innocent longer. We find it hard to learn from trial

and error, difficult to apply a past lesson to a new problem, and virtually impossible really to know when we are being teased, taken advantage of or misled.

Closer to now than I would like to admit, I was totally taken advantage of by one of my employers. I made the mistake of assuming the man was just and honorable simply because his company is largely philanthropic. It never dawned on me that someone would help others for profit and a prestigious title. I was mistaken. In the end, I was not too banged up, just cheated of a few thousand dollars and my ideals. But what if something else had gone wrong? Could I have been talked into being a part of the game plan that took money from others without their realizing it? Could I have been convinced to join my employer in his get rich quick schemes without realizing the wrongs I would have been committing? I worry that I certainly could have. The lesson I learned from that incident tainted me some. It made me look at others who hold positions of authority and prestige through suspicious lenses. Are they who they say they are, I always ask myself? Will they lead me astray, I wonder? Help me figure this one out, I ask my husband or my family. And so they do. I ask, they help me think my way through the NT maze.

But what if your aspie tends toward silence and mystery? What if they are reluctant to share their impressions, their concerns and their days in the main? Life on the front might be easier for everyone to manage and happier to control, but is it less worrisome? Not at all. Less embarrassing? Probably, but is it worth the price you'll pay for not knowing what goes on in the aspie's thoughts? Worries over the hidden world of the aspie are often the kind of concerns that fray logic and leave easy understanding in the dust. I rather believe this occurs largely because the aspie sense of life relies on experiences and patterns that are markedly different from the NT's understanding of why and how. While the aspies do not try to fool the neurotypicals at their own game, while they do not intend to be deceiving or evasive, they can indeed spin a tangled skein. Misunderstandings can build upon misunderstandings until no one can figure out where anything began or where anything will end. Arguments can ensue, mistrusts will be fostered and wham – the aspie can become a lost and lonely reclusive afraid to work with the NT world again. Then again, the reasons behind the quiet can come from a very different well, a safe and sure well. For example, the aspie might not understand it is important to share his thoughts. He may see absolutely no point in disclosing anything other than a few tidbits now and then. He might like the world of silence, the world of the mist. Or he might not speak because he has learned that when he talks, others do too. It might be the voices of others he does not want to hear. Then again, he might not speak because to do so causes too much anxiety, too many struggles with too many emotions.

If I had such an aspie in my life, I would do what I could to respect her silence, yet I would surely try to communicate with her, just in a different manner. I would suggest we both learn, or make up our own, sign language. I would try using art or drama or music or dance to talk to one another. The only thing I would try very hard to insist on would be that the aspie find some way, if at all possible, to let me know if something unpleasant came too near. 'Something unpleasant,' I would tell her, 'is anything that upsets you or makes you uncertain about what you should do next. Unpleasant does not have to be something that harms or hurts, it can just be something that makes you anxious or confused.'

By my definition, unpleasant covers a lot of ground. I think it has to. It is better to err on the side of too much than not enough, at least in this case. I cannot rest if I think my child is facing a world made up of crazy proportions. I have to be certain she has formed a rational and safe image of the things that come her way, be they good or bad. Everything from the little such as her thinking she has made a new friend when in fact the 'new friend' wants nothing to do with her – to the big that leads her to

believe it is acceptable to cheat on a test because she misunderstood her teacher's sarcasm when he said, 'Oh well, if you didn't
study for the test go ahead and copy off of your neighbors.' She
needs our ever vigilant attention until we know for a fact she can
avoid such pitfalls on her own.

Misunderstandings seem to rule our lives. Though I am now
at the point at which I can appear to be in-sync with the rest of
the crowd, I never am. Never. I notice too much. I see every detail
of every inch of every person's body and all that surrounds them
all at once until looking at them is like looking at someone
caught in a wind tunnel. Body parts move too fast. Eyes twitch
on and off, on and off. Shoulders sway and pitch and shudder.
Feet tap, hands run, heads bob. I hear too much. Teeth
clak-clak-click together. Sprinkles of spittle splash into the little
pockets that rim the lips. Words come out twinged and tweaked
too fast or too slow or too crisp or too fat. I know too little. Small
talk rules slip from my fingers. I lose track of the conversation's
point. I try too hard to pretend.

I wish I could ask people to share written dialogues with me. I
could relate to that. The layers would be peeled back and only
the important would reach out to be held. I could talk to people
better if we didn't have to talk. In fact, it would be so very easy
for me to turn off and turn away from most things conversa-
tional. My aspie father is much the same way. I always picture
him sitting on his side of our couch watching the TV news
reports or working on his engineering problems. Quietly, he
would concentrate. Homed in, he would be − centered,
grounded, and steady on that which made sense to him. Outside
noises and commotion seemed to roll off him like water runs off
a duck's back. He didn't let the outside in, even when it knocked.
Literally. Countless times he would sit and stare straight ahead as
a visitor knocked and knocked on our door. Despite the fact that
the visitors could see my father through the window, despite the
fact that they would yell, 'Hello? Mr. Holliday? Hello?' he sat
and stared. He wasn't being rude. He was just tuned-out. When I

would go and answer the door myself, Dad would extend a warm welcome and a how-do-you-do to the visitor, though that was all he would usually say. When I asked my father why he didn't talk to people much, he would answer 'I don't see the point in talking to anyone if I'm not going to learn anything.' I can relate to that. But then again, I understand that small talk does have a purpose. That kind of talk can work to pass time, camouflage nervous tension, lay a foundation for new friendships, and keep serious or painful conversations and thoughts safely at bay. That kind of talk can help people connect. On its own though, it doesn't necessarily help the typical aspie connect. We need to be taught to appreciate and understand it.

MAKING SENSE OF SMALL TALK

○ By its very nature, small talk will not always thrill or delight. Knowing this ahead of the game will greatly reduce the chances of the aspie saying something a bit too bold, like, 'Don't you have anything interesting to talk about?' Or my favorite, 'What makes you think I want to hear any of this?' Teach the aspies among you this cardinal rule 'think it but do not say it.' Tell them it is acceptable to admit to themselves that a particular conversation is too tedious for their taste, but instill within them the realization that it is rarely necessary to share that thought with the speaker. Point out to them that nothing good will come from such an admission, no matter how true.

○ Explain the fact that small talk is often just a volley of niceties between people, that it is not something which demands a great deal of creative thought or much of an intellectual commitment and naturally, not something anyone must engage in for any length of time. Role play situations where small talk is likely to be called on; for example, at a social gathering, a waiting line or any event where people are gathered in one spot. Think about simple and short phrases the aspie could memorize and then use when wanting to get away from small talk without appearing rude or impetuous. Take turns adding polite and nice sentiments to a cumulative list you can turn to for reviewing and role playing whenever the need arises. Possible statements could include: 'Well, it's been nice talking to you. Good bye now.' 'Oops, look at the time. I had better be on my way.' 'Thanks for the conversation. Take care.' Be certain and explain that once these kinds of statements are issued, it is appropriate and necessary for the aspie to then turn and move her body away from the speaker as a last sign that the conversation is over.

o Role play what happens to a conversation when someone verbally walks all over other people's conversations. Using logic, illustrate how hard it is to know what someone else intends to say if their conversation is cut off in midstream. Point out, through example, that any sentence or thought cannot be understood if it is not heard in its entirety. Then role play situations where the aspie is interrupted during speaking. Talk about how annoying it is to have a statement cut short.

o Again using logic, prove to the aspie how essential it is that the speaker build his conversation around appropriate transitions in the conversation. Write several mock conversations in a notebook leaving plenty of room after each one for comments and reviews. Let some of the conversations follow regular transitions and let some come as if from the sky. For example, the appropriate conversations might go something like this, 'I really am enjoying this day. Cool weather really wakes me up. Warm weather, on the other hand, is stifling to me. I know the flowers and trees look prettier in the summer, but give me a hard freeze any day!' On the other hand, an inappropriately transitioned statement might sound like this, 'I really am enjoying this day. Cool weather really wakes me up. I hate to go fishing. I want pizza for dinner. What time is it?' Ask the aspie to write down what each conversation is about in the space provided beneath each one. If they have done a proper analysis, the inappropriately transitioned statements will be described by a longer list of topics. Point out the fact that the conversation holding the fewest number of topics is the easiest to follow and contribute to.

o Role play the kinds of scenes that would be likely to confuse or upset the aspie, but do this in the quiet and safe calm of the home. Let the aspie run through life as an actor runs through dress rehearsals. Taking on the role of employer, personal friend, teacher, mailman, retail clerk, waitress, etc., lead the aspie through the kinds of conversations and scenarios they would likely have with these people.

o Help the aspie understand the nature of rhetorical versus real questions. Explain that a rhetorical such as, 'How are you?' is the kind of question a casual friend or stranger would ask rather than simply smiling and saying hello. Explain these kinds of rhetorical statements and questions demand only a quick and short reply as opposed to a completely truthful answer. On the other hand, make certain the aspie knows this kind of question is not always rhetorical. Such would be the case, for example, if it were asked by someone, say a physician or employer, who really does want to know the essential answers to the question. Try to help the aspie understand when a question is rhetorical and when it is not by getting the aspie to make 'who said what to whom' matches. To accomplish this, you might say a rhetorical to an aspie and then have him think of the kinds of people who would want a full and actual answer to it. To make this more entertaining, you could write a variety of rhetoricals on note cards and a variety of speakers on separate notecards. Then, playing a game of matching, the aspie could couple up the statement cards with people who really do want an answer. The left over cards would represent people who did not want a full answer. To check the aspie's understanding, play the reverse of the game and ask them to match up who would not want a full answer with a particular question. Note, this time, that the left over speaker cards represent people who would want a real answer.

o Show videotapes of good quality movies that accurately illustrate group dynamics and social situations, then discuss, compare, contrast and learn how small talk acted as a helpful catalyst for friendship and shared time together.

When properly learned and put into practice, small talk can be a comfortable tool to keep in a social skills survival toolbox. We need as many tools as we can get, for the more tools, the better the odds of surviving successfully and happily. Tom and I want our girls to understand the dynamics of society's language through in and through out, so they can go beyond complacency and on toward an appreciation of all kinds of communication formulae from secret keeping to small talking. The more they know, the more they will become.

4

Running for Cover

In a cottage, by a shore, the world seems right.
The outside stays beyond the blanket walls.
The soul can wrap itself snug and warm, safe and sure.
The body can breathe.
The thoughts can rest in the space held tight.
Inside a cottage, by a shore, the world seems right.

My aspie friends often refer to the world as if it were a crazed maze. I understand why they think that. Just when we think we have figured out how to behave, how to read people, how to fit in and how to learn NT ways and means, we smack into yet another new hallway that will wind us to more closed doors and dead ends. If only NTs would stay firm in the way they do things and in their expectations of others, we aspies think to ourselves, perhaps then we could catch on to their ways, once and for all. But as this world of ours is fluid and not static, we aspies will be compelled, at some point or other, to try and roll with the tide as best we can. Sounds easy. Isn't easy. No matter how easy and effortless some of we aspies make it seem, there is nothing the slightest bit easy about navigating your way through a world you are not intrinsically keyed-in to understand. It is a constant effort on our part to remain whole and happy. Of course it is an effort well worth the cost and not an effort unheard of in the course of human existence. Everyone struggles. It's just that our struggles never seem to go completely away. Frustration mounts when we discover we are lost yet again. Wildly, we run down the hallway of our maze banging into the walls that keep us from looking over the edge to see what we're missing and where we should be. Fear grabs us by the ankles, yanking us down until we have wrapped ourselves into a tiny little ball stuffed against a corner of a lost path. Anxiety fills our body with crawly things that cannot be reached from the outside so that no matter how much we jump up and down and scratch and scream, the crawlies continue their race up and down our bones. When I am overwhelmed by the frustration and the fear and the anxiety, I run for cover. Only when my heart has stopped racing and my mind has quit spinning, can I set my mind to go fetch the intelligence and logic it will need to get me free of the maze.

Lots of things put me in the maze. Crowds with their rumbles and roars and their pushing and shelving of people against people in tight passageways, long lines and seats smashed too close together…bright lights and things that move too quickly past my eyes and virtually any smell beyond the soft scent of a baby…broken rules, courtesies ignored, helpless people shoved out of the way of the big and the strong, egos running amuck… double standards, two-facedness, false pretenses, dishonesty, cheating, lying and all of their ugly cousins… These are the kinds of things that leave me inconsolable, stir my exasperation and snap my mind shut. No matter how many times I come face to face with one of those lurid incidents, I react the same. I will fixate and perseverate on the unnaturalness of the thing or the ugliness of the experience or the inanity of the behavior. On and on and on I will blather, struggling all the while to figure out the reasons behind the surroundings and the actions. It is never enough for me just to accept things at face value or even to accept that some things have no explanation. I have to dig and seek until I am mentally exhausted. Scenarios play in my mind like a bad drama with me as the director trying to construct some sort of logical pattern to the chaos before me.

I think this would be a great pattern of thinking, if I could restrict it to significant issues. But I can't. I re-think and overanalyze even the most mind numbing of things. Let's say, for example, that someone told me they hated to wear pants with pleats in them. No big deal. Pretty innocuous statement that certainly doesn't involve my day-to-day life. Now, let's say I see that same person wearing pants with pleats in them. In my mind, I'll circulate explanations for the pants. Maybe, I'll think, someone told the person she looked thinner in pants with pleats. Maybe they were a gift from someone she cares about and so she feels obligated to wear them. Perhaps they are an old pair of pants, ones she had stashed in the closet from some time when she did like pleated pants and now she's wearing them because to ignore them would be a waste of clothing. Or, I'll ponder, maybe she told me she didn't like pleated pants because she heard me say I didn't like them and she's just trying to make me feel comfortable. Maybe she's copying my tastes and me. Or maybe she's trying to fool me into wearing these kinds of pants so I'll look out of style. Could it be she is lying to me for some reason? Is she two-faced or a fair-weather friend? Might it be she is just a goofy sort who speaks without thinking? Spiraling, circling, around my mind goes, until I have run it ragged. Quickly, good sense frays and paranoia gathers speed. Rationale gets tossed aside, even as logic fights to stay. And all this over a pair of pants.

When I am out and about with the public, I pretend that this sort of mental rambling is the farthest thing from my mind. I tell only my very closest friends and my family when I think my thoughts are getting too wild and uncontrolled. I don't let on to my obsessions or my perseverations. I keep them far from the eyes of most who know me. This is particularly true of my perseverations. I rather think minds like mine frighten people from the NT land. I think they don't know quite what to say to me sometimes, maybe for fear that they'll set off one of my perseverations and one of my long and twisted mental shifts. I suppose when people hear me articulate my thoughts, no matter how logical they are, they are left to wonder if I am just a bit too close to crazy. Some seem unable to understand that the mind can get stuck running round a wheel in chase of an obsessive thought. While this kind of thinking comes perfectly naturally to me, my experience tells me it is not at all typical for the NT population. NTs seem quite able to blow-off thoughts that disrupt their line of reasoning. I am not so fortunate. When I enter the perseveration stage, I know there is a very good chance I will run ragged until I drop. I used to give in to that fall. Or perhaps I was simply unable to avoid it. No matter. The point is, I can't blank out any more. Too many people depend on me these days. Now when the mazes threaten to become totally over-whelming perseverations, I straight away head toward my home, the only place on earth where I can settle in, and be and do exactly what I please and exactly what I need, in order to overcome the perseverations heading my way and the anxiety that will surely follow on their tail.

It is not at all hard to design an aspie home. Neither a degree nor an ardent interest in interior design is necessary to the design. It is necessary however, for the aspie to have a good un-derstanding of the colors and geometrics that make him feel balanced. For some of us, this knowledge is as blatant to us as is the color of our eyes. For other aspies, these notions may sit hidden on a very subconscious level. Those aspies will need to experiment with color swatches, textures, tight and open spaces, and temperature controls and light sources to formulate what kinds of elements they need to create a safe haven.

In good aspie form, I begin my sanctuary analysis by looking at small pieces of the whole environment, one by one by one. If I were to try and figure out how to arrange my home in one fell swoop, from top to bottom and front to back, I would be blinded by the choices and stuck by the decisions. Instead, I start with something rather simple. For me, this means color. Color is the easiest place to start and the easiest thing to change. Color is a cheap fix, a fast fix, and a very emotionally satisfying fix. Which color? Hard to say. Research is inconclusive in its attempts to determine which color suits those on the autistic spectrum best. I tend to believe it is an individual choice, a variable not shared on a universal basis by all affected with autism. Blue is the answer to my needs. Blue shades envelop me in their coolness, making the world seem slowed down and centered. Blue acts as a sensory shield for me, making shadows and light and peripheral visions wait their turn for my attention. Things do not invade my consciousness when I am surrounded by blue. I feel as if I can melt into my blues. Cool colors. Cool colors sigh. Hot colors scream. They are not to my liking in big chunks, though I have grown to appreciate them when they wink here and there among my cools. They act as surprises to me, like wake up calls that stir up my senses and tickle my ribs. Sometimes hot colors are sparks of good things. Handy things. For me.

My aspie daughter likes blue, but she yearns for yellow. Hot shades are her quick elixir, particularly the shades of yellow. From the moment she was able to assert her preferences on things like color and clothing, yellow was her first choice. Most of the time it has been her only choice and believe you me, until very recently, life was not pleasant for the person who forgot that rule. I vividly remember my aspie throwing a beautiful new outfit her grandmother had given her straight into the trash can because it was pink. Pink is the color her twin wears, not her! I remember my mother getting the outfit out of the trash and attempting to get my daughter to see how pretty it was. No Ma'am. Back into the trash the outfit went over and over again until it was decided the outfit would be returned. Smart move. Tenacity runs deep in the aspie...

My other family members are split in their devotion to the cool or hot parts of the color wheel. So, in the main, I chose to paint our world around plenty of blue and plenty of yellow.

Many of our walls are blue. Many of our furnishings are yellow. We mix other colors in, but only as subtle friends, not pushy bosses. For the rest of our home, we have found soft white, soft taupe and soft beige to be kind backdrops for our scheme. Those colors seem to upset none of us, though neither do they entice us. They just are. Perhaps it would be wiser in terms of my daughter's and my own emotional health if we drenched every scene with blue or yellow, but I have my doubts. I tend to think our most craved colors serve each of us better when they come in spits and bits. I worry that too much of a good thing will tempt us too close to the flame. If we grow too dependent on our colors for calming, if we become too enmeshed with them for safety, will it then follow we cannot function successfully without them? Seen from another view, if we take on too much of our perfect color, will that color lose its influence and its strength somewhere down the road? And if it does, what would become of our quick and close refuge if we hadn't developed an interest and longing for a substituted color? Would our safety net be filled with holes? Of course, these are no more than shaky hypotheses on my part, but because the possible ramifications run so deep, I decide to go with my instinct. Beige for the main, but our chosen colors for the little cottages by the sea we carve out of our everyday home.

If color is like water to us aspies, symmetry in design is our magic elixir. Obviously, this is not something the average homebuyer can play with – we find a home we can afford and we hope for the best. Striving for something more reasonable, I try to think instead in terms of weight made real by texture, furniture design, pictures and other elements I can add or take away in any spot, in any room. Rather than symmetry being defined as squares set off by matching squares, I think metaphorically in terms of a balanced scale. A room has to *feel* balanced, not be truly balanced. Real symmetry of standing wall angles comes as a huge bonus, but not a necessary essential. Instead, I rely on furniture and accessory arranging to represent the tradition of symmetry. Bookcases can be precisely arranged to make the book lines clean and straight. Pictures can be put in centers of walls while two exact chairs can be set one across from the other. Exact candles displayed in matching candleholders can be anchored one across the other with some single accessory element in between. So it goes. But beyond the placement of things, what can we do? Designers tell us to use our sensory emotions to gauge the weight of the rest of our environmental influences. Match heavy things with heavy. Not in terms of raw weight, but in terms of a look – a feel. For instance, you could make a heavy leather couch a better match for a not-so-heavy Shaker style spindle chair by tossing a thick and substantial throw or comforter over the back of the chair. You could balance a window covered with slight and billowy curtains by putting small black and white photos on the wall directly across from the window. Light matches light, heavy matches heavy. Accessories, furnishings and textures become key players that can make established home walls seem less visible and then, less demonstrative and dictating. Without a proper sense of balance, things in a room breathe into life and become zealous fiends that strangle.

The need for self-defined order more than passes through my aspie's environment. Luckily for her, she has her own room to control. If she could not perseverate on what went where in her room, I know for certain that she would perseverate on what went where throughout the house. In fact, if she is allowed, she will indeed re-arrange our things, even the things of friends in their home, until they fit within her framework for order. Knowing this about my daughter, my husband and I are able to direct her attention from the things in her environment we know she would find chaotic. We are able to tell her before she heads off to school that it is not up to her to tell the teacher how to arrange the classroom and not up to her to re-organize her friends' lockers. We warn her to turn her gaze from any mess or clump of disarray that would likely send her straight to an obsession for order. We tell her she can talk about needing more symmetry and organization, but that she cannot act on that need until she is home and safe to do so. We warn her to look for the bump in her road, we tell her how to steer clear from it, and then we tell her how to get back on track. For now, that seems all we can do for her...unless she smashes into the bump head on. Should our aspie give in to her impulses and cross the line into someone else's territory, to re-do, re-situate and re-structure their disarray, we gently guide her back to a safe spot so she can come full circle. We will listen while she rants about how horrible the situation was before she fixed it up; we will listen while she tells us how wrong it is to be messy; we will listen while she expresses shock over the fact that the person she cleaned up dared to show anger at her intervention; and we will hold her when she whispers through her tears that she did not mean to make anyone mad, that she was only trying to help them make things right again. And then we will hold our breath and quietly go back to the beginning of our circle knowing we will have to revisit this situation over and over and over again, for as many times as it takes until our aspie tames her desire to organize those things she calls 'a mess.'

When I see young children and adolescents misbehaving in public, I think about my daughter's dismay in the face of that which she calls 'a mess.' Then, I give them the benefit of the doubt before I commit them to the Kingdom of Brat. I am convinced these distraught folks sense they are about to be gobbled up by the room or the area they are enclosed in. While it is doubtful they can explain any of this to their resolute caretakers, a close look at their actions should say more than enough. Despite all the pleading and threatening, they will do everything in their power to stay as clear of that area they see as frighteningly off-center, uneven and uncertain. They might grab a wall for balance, flop to the floor as if to crawl or bolt in the other direction. They sense the chill and they fear that if they step one foot in the locale, they will be chewed to mush.

I know this feeling well. It happens to me all the time. It happened just yesterday… Hungry for a snack, my kids asked me to go to a general department store in our area to buy them each one of those monster sized pretzels that come to you fresh from the oven. This is an easy thing to get me to do, because I love those salty knots of bread just as much as anyone does. The kids waited in the car with their dad while I made my way into the store. Nonchalantly I walked toward the snack area pondering how much the pretzels were likely to cost, how many napkins I would need to get and how many packets of mustard I would ask for. My focus so entertained, I didn't notice the patterns coming toward me until it was too late. Black and white waxy floor tiles patched the ground. Lipstick red chairs with silver legs dotted the room. Mirrors covered the walls. Enough lights to light up a runway, lit up the counter where my pretzels sat. Had I seen what was coming from a safe distance, I would have stopped, stared off for a minute or two to compose my thoughts and prepare my mind for the onslaught of so many busy pieces. I would have spoken to myself, no doubt loud enough for anyone near me to hear, telling me the floor wasn't really moving, the lights wouldn't really sear me and the dots of red wouldn't bounce against me. I would have told myself to take charge of my thoughts and remember my goal – warm, fat pretzels. My motivation for the yummy would have helped me ease the strain, and whatever nerves were left unchecked would have been reined in by deep breaths and the lecture I would force myself to hear.

But of course, I hadn't been paying attention. The ramshackled room struck me like an angry snake. I froze, stunned. In shock, I stared straight ahead. A few people passed by me, most likely thinking I had paused to read the menu overhead. There was nothing in my demeanor to suggest otherwise. I wasn't screaming or tantruming or stomping my feet, not on the outside. I am, after all, a grown adult who knows full well how to let that which bothers me plague me and no one else. Had I been a little person, I am absolutely certain I would have been doing more than screaming, tantruming and stomping my feet. And I am certain nothing could have dragged me in that room without each of those behaviors following.

After I don't know how many minutes in Limbo, I finally managed to find the three keys I look for when I am about to freak-out: reassurance, motivation and patience. I gave myself a mental break and told myself it was OK to hate the scene in front of me, that it was natural for me to balk, that it was fine if I took a few more minutes to compose myself. I took in the smell of the warm pretzels and reminded myself how good they would taste and how happy the kids would be when I gave them one to munch on. Willing myself to move, ever slowly and purposefully, I covered the thirty feet between the prize and myself. I stared at the fry machine and asked the cook for five pretzels, please.

That was the best pretzel I have had yet. It couldn't have been better if I had made it from wheat I had planted and harvested myself. Even small rewards stand tall when a stumbling block is overcome.

The aspie home, blended to the aspie's needs, can provide an atmosphere of calm, confidence and focus; the very things we need if we are to climb toward our potential. Only one element I know of goes farther than the most perfect aspie house in the world can to help many of us find ourselves. It is a simple thing that requires very little space, funds or talent to design. It is a spot.

Walk with me for awhile back to the world of childhood, and see the castles you created out of cardboard, the forts you made from twigs and rocks, and the hidden hideaways you made from clumps of bushes. I can see them, with intensity and a poignant longing. I see my invariable attempts to create special areas made for me and me alone. I see myself turning lawn chairs and beach towels into a fortress that held everything but curious crawling creatures from my world. I take deep, comforting breaths as my memory takes me beneath the waters of my pool so I can again visit my precious pretend sea friends who would whisper my existence but never shout my whereabouts. I kick back my heels imagining myself back up on a high, thick branch of our big maple tree where it seemed I sat at the top of a grand set of stairs that led to a fantastical world no one but me could enter. I feel my body go flat as a pancake just as it used to when I would squirrel my way beneath my bed until I fit snugly between the crevices left by my headboard's form. I can still curl my legs tight until I'm a little ball small enough to sit sandwiched between the stacked lunchroom tables that, when put on end, resembled cubbyholes made to order for small, quiet kids. I can see myself sneaking behind corners, my mother's legs and curtains. I remember too well, for now the image brings a shudder to my mind, wandering down manholes, and venturing through dense, dank woodlands. I did then, what I often do now, though in different forms… I sought a unique refuge from the world of others. A place where I could stim if I needed, yodel if I liked, talk to myself without being interrupted or sit in the stillness if I so chose. Then, just as now, it was important to feel enclosed, smack in the midst of something strong and compressed. Spaces. Niches. Cubicles. My spot is my nook. My vacation home away from, though still within, my everyday home.

Just like their mom, two of my girls carve out nooks for themselves when the situation lures them to fold in and curl up. Is this alcove business really an essential for aspies? I trust so. In fact, I believe it to be so for my mostly NT people, too. Perhaps for everyone. Consider. Bears have their caves tucked away in their forest home. Goldfish suspend their float behind a rock, otherwise lost in a big bowl. Dogs make cozy dens in their master's homes. Most creatures, it could be pointed out, seem prone to alcoves carved out of their vast environment. Is it so unusual then to see our home as a place where we might all need to carve out our own spot?

A spot. Our own spot. How to define? To begin with, a spot does not need to be an elaborately appointed spacious area within a mansion. Space and finances are not the most essential basics necessary for creating our inner sanctuaries. No, we do not have to have a cottage by a shore. We do not even have to have an office or a guestroom or a space in a converted attic. A safe spot is simply an enclosed area set off by very visual place markers. It can be as big as, or in my case, as small as, it need be. In making our own spot, we need our imagination to guide us to possibility as well as a willing ability to forgo standard expectations and typical restraints. In short, we need to work with what we have. We need to explore and discover. We need to think and do.

How can we do this? How can we work from what we have to make it what we need? As much as I would like it to be so, my home will never be a series of symmetrically laid out rooms set up to allow both connection between groups, and isolation for individuals. Our home is set up first as a family retreat for, despite our AS, we have a need for cohesion which, though not as great as our need for individuality, is none the less very much an essential part of our whole. In this family, we tend to be as much defined by our own being as we are by our collective grouping. Today, our home reflects that reality. We eat from the same refrigerator, cook off the same stove and eat at a common dinner table. We read our books and play our games around the same fire. We plant in the same yard. Then, whenever we need and whenever it is possible, we create our own mini-home within our family home. Bedrooms become our cottages. Quiet, hidden alcoves become our shores. Corners become nooks that hold us tight until we feel strong enough to begin again.

SMALL SPOT MAKING

Anywhere. The intent is not to design a new room, but a small area for calming, something not a whole lot bigger than a body sized spot. Any safe cranny will do. In our home, we have several special spots. I tend toward an alcove under my desk. One of my girls enjoys an area beneath her elevated platform bed and another prefers the top of her bunk bed. All the girls gravitate to an area beneath the stairs we had carpeted, painted and lighted specifically so the hideaway would be very accessible. This area, the favorite in the house, is gotten to through either a main door off a storage way, or by crawling through what looks like a cabinet, but is really a hidden passageway to the area. Even adults cannot resist going into the area through the cabinet.

Obviously, this addition to the house was not totally inexpensive, though it could have been. Instead of actually dry walling the area off, we could have elected to hang inexpensive sheets or shower curtains to create make-shift walls. Forgoing carpet, we could have laid down an old blanket or inexpensive carpet remnant, or tile squares or vinyl floor scraps. No matter the finished details, the point remains: the area is a perfect spot to build the aspie spot. If stairs are not part of your home's design, look elsewhere. Get on your knees and look around from a lowered area of vision. You will be likely to see the world as you might have when you were a child free from the schematics that guide your sensibilities now that you are an adult. A corner, a window seat, the area beneath stairs, a closet, a tree house, a clean large dog house, the area beneath a table, a shower enclosure, a small pop-up tent, an empty and large appliance box, the area behind a door. You get the picture. Think warm and cozy and you will be thinking about a perfect spot.

Once you have your spot's locale figured out, find a way to bring music to it. Classical music works wonders for us. So does music from the sounds of nature. Decorate the area with posters of the aspie's favorite characters or hobbies. Add a basket filled with favorite stim toys. Spray the area with a favorite scent. Light the room, if you can, with a colored bulb that is close to the aspie's favorite color. Put a pad of paper or a board made for writing on, to encourage the aspie to be introspective when they most need to be – the times they turn to their spot for comfort. And remember the cardinal rule: a spot needs to be free from criticism, free from unwanted visitors (unless safety concerns need to be met) and totally respected for what it is – a refuge on demand.

With the background dropped, the aspie home can become what it needs to be. A refuge for the family to support one another, learn from one another and when necessary, hide from one another! That's right. Hide. If I am honest and true, I have to say every member of our family has the right to vanish from view the moment they feel they have to. I think every family needs that right guaranteed them, but I feel it is essential for a family with any kind of special need to carve that guarantee into stone.

If I am falling beyond my control, I will be the first to tell my children to leave me to my quiet time so I can more quickly move myself to the mom that will help them bake cookies and play games. As I become more familiar with myself, I find it becomes easier and easier for me to know when I am facing overload, and easier every day to gauge what kinds of things preclude my overloading. I can now use my logic to tell my kids why I need to use my sanctuary to keep my stress from overpowering my good mommy traits. I used to be ashamed of the notion that I was not always the stereotypical pearl wearing, sweet smiling, mom-of-lore.

Now I realize no child's caretaker ever manages the role with complete accuracy. Better I confess my weakness to my kids so they can have the chance to provide me with the chance I need to find my way back to the good mom that loves to be with them on center stage. Experience and my explanations have taught them when I head to my room or my office, I am heading toward my symbolic cottage. They know to let me go. When they can. Sometimes they cannot resist following me about, telling me which sister hit whom, which sister ignored what and which sister had better stop bugging whom or else! On these days, I do what any savvy parent would do. I hide. I go to one or two of my most secret places the kids have yet to discover. Oh, they are in the house close enough to the main so I can still hear every word the kids are screaming at one another, but far enough away to keep me from them long enough for me to regroup. I go to my secret spot, assume a relaxed position, close my eyes, breathe deep and hum or sing or count over and over to twelve and back. I de-stress. Not at all an unusual response to a charged atmosphere. Well, unless crawling under a bed or cramming myself into the corner of my closet is unusual. To me, it is as normal as lying back in a lounge chair on a hot sunny day.

This trick of mine, this hiding without encouraging seeking, is one I have directly passed down to my children. A trick they have mastered beyond my ability to do so. They can find the most interesting hiding places. The only rules – they must tell me where they are if I start counting to ten, and they must not go near any danger. They cannot hide by a furnace or in a washer or dryer or the attic or any place that takes away oxygen or any place that presents with fire or sharp objects or potentially harmful fumes. This system of ours works well virtually every time we use it. *Virtually* every time.

One evening we lost a child, our almost aspie child. I knew from the moment this child got home from school something had not gone well in her day. Sure enough when I asked the two visible girls what happened to their now vanished sister, the story spilled out. 'Mom! She got bit at school and she had to go to the principal's office!'

'Hmmm…are you sure? The principal did not call me to mention this. Are you sure she did not get into trouble in some other way? Are you sure she wasn't involved in something she shouldn't have been?' After all, vanishing kids make their moms and dads suspicious.

'No Mom. She did not do anything. She just got bit.'

Unable to believe my daughter would be invisible because she had been a victim and not a persecutor, I called the principal only to have the sisters' story legitimized. Yes, this child had been bitten; no she had not been in trouble herself. My mind ticking, I asked the principal how my daughter had reacted to the principal's insistence she come to her office – beginning to suspect the invitation was not at all well received or even understood by my child. Sure enough, the principal admitted to sensing some apprehension in my child's demeanor. Some? I told the principal we could not find our child and that I would in the future appreciate a call whenever any of my girls were her visitors, no matter the reason, for chances were good my girls would not clearly see the reason on their own. My aggravation thus spent on the lackadaisical principal, I began to worry my little girl was on her way to the big, bad woods with her teddy and a peanut butter sandwich in tow. Truly. We lived in the midst of an old quarry-turned-neighborhood at the time, and I knew only too well poisonous snakes and hidden sink holes would bring nothing but harm to my child who no doubt thought these dangers would be less risky than the eyes of a mother who thought she had done wrong. For two hours we searched, yelled, and wandered inside and out. To our collective dismay, we could not find the daughter, our almost aspie who is so quiet and so prone to withdrawal, especially when she misunderstands her world.

Frightened beyond words we decided it was time to call for official help when miraculously down the steps came this little one, safe, sleepy eyed and hungry. It turned out she had crawled into a tight corner of her sister's walk-in closet and hidden her tiny body beneath a mound of sister's fallen clothes like a bear cub does just as winter sets in. Hibernating. That is what this one had been doing. So able was she to shut out and down, she was able to ignore our insisting she come out. The rules stand firm these days. 'No sleeping while hiding,' now goes without saying.

Hibernating, hiding, sneaking off...they are all about control; an essential need of the aspie. While the outside world often thwarts our sense of control, it seems the least we can hope for is control within our home structure. A desire for control is as innately natural to the aspie as is her notion to perseverate. Control is a big sail on our ship. When it is flying freely, we take great joy in commanding it along side of (and sometimes in spite of) the wind's most clear-cut direction. Of course, it is not always possible to shout, 'I am in charge here!' Would that it were, for when something happens to stifle the way we employ and enforce our sense of control, storms are virtually certain to brew.

In NT terms, control is something people are awarded following a supervised tenure with every day trial and error, general experience, maturity and proof of intellect and abilities. But in AS terms, control is something we instantaneously need, covet and demand. Control. A powerful emotion. An emotion best respected. A feeling we aspies have that needs to be culti-vated and gently guided within the understanding supervision of people who care deeply about our mental energies and our sense of serenity. When we have learnt to respect it, control – at least over who we are, what we do and how we choose to live – can encourage the AS person to be intelligently assertive, posi-tively confident and gently tenacious. For if we learn to respect and work with our desire to control our elements, maybe, just maybe, it will follow we will be more likely and able to find respite among the fury and the sounds of the world beyond our own. However, if left to orbit on its own, our desire to control not so much our destiny, but our here and now, can turn us into pig-headed, demonstrative shovers who make impudent demands and who place unreasonable mandates on every aspect of our being and our relating. Within the proper framework, then, our sense of control over our main environment seems to be the least offensive and least problematic way for us aspies safely to establish a setting wherein we can exercise our innate desire for sameness and routine and structure and order. It is a way to make things right among the chaos of too many sights and smells and textures. This ability to call our own shots in our own sanctuary, might just be what we all need to keep ourselves on a more even keel, particularly when we find ourselves in a situation (most of life) wherefrom we cannot assert much control at all.

A tight sense of control seems to keep a cozy lid on out-of-control situations and behavior-bound problems. That being the case, control lends itself to our being better able to sharpen our focus and organize our mental framework. Control, focus, a clear mental framework – just more of the qualities we need in order to get us through the NT world and its expecta-tions.

So it goes for me, so it goes for my aspie daughter. I am afraid we are not much use to anyone if we are left to free-fall our way through the world all the time, every day. The question becomes, how much control do we need in order to keep us balanced? Im-possible to say for sure. As with most things in life, the answer is highly variable; some will need more sense of control and some will need less.

In my family, each of us has total control over his or her spot. In that spot, each of us has the freedom to make an area look, smell and feel like whatever he or she wishes. For two of my daughters, smell is a big issue. Perfumes lie on the air in their rooms with a heaviness I could never learn to appreciate. So, too, are their rooms filled with artificial lights and music and an almost always turned on computer and a hill of clothes worthy of a mountain climber's attention. Their rooms are not rooms this aspie can relax or revel in. They are too complex in their chaos. Things sift out from every corner, under every furnishing and behind every drawer in random arrangements. My aspie daughter is neat and regimented and organized and concrete in her placement of her objects, which will stay exactly where she put them day after day after day. Like many aspies, she has a strong need for sameness, especially in her own environment. The clothes sit where they belong in her closet, the books snuggle on their shelves and the toys sit in perfect rows organized by sensible categories. Needless to say, this child's room is far more inviting to me than are her sisters'. My husband claims the spare room as his den. In it he can catalog his papers, keep his tidy golf collections, and store his oxfords and his khakis in groupings separated according to winter and summer wear. His closet and his bathroom are on a floor completely separate from mine. We learned long ago that my stuff and his could not coexist as well as their owners could. My room is suited to fit me. I have my blues and my architecture prints and my hills of magazines and books that are nearly as high as my messy daughters' mountains of clothes. My room, though rarely conventionally neat, is tidy to me. Everything, at least, is put into stacks. Books go in one corner, dirty clothes on my couch, clean clothes get hung according to color schemes in the closet, make-up gets tossed into one bag, and so it goes…new categories of mountains crop up as often as new stuff makes its way into my room.

If our home were not designed so that every one of us could have separate bedrooms, we would do the next best thing. We would assign everyone pieces of the home where they could do what they willed. This might mean everyone had nothing more than a bookcase, display case, desk or even set of cardboard boxes to call their own, but they would at least have something. Control. We have to control our environment. Even if just a tiny part of it.

My mind often wanders to a world where none of us has to leave our house, where each of us could do all we needed from within the four walls of our own rooms and our own spots. In this world, it would be possible to keep chaos at bay and peace at hand. No one would interfere with the rights and privileges of others and no one would step on anyone's senses. Every home would be a cottage and every spot would be a refuge. In this world, all of us, even we aspies, would be happy.

5

Daring to be Different

The mighty wind smiled as she dipped down to embrace the tiny sparrow. The trees let go a heavy wail. Never, thought they, would a bird of such small significance be so tenderly adopted by one as strong as the wind. The wind, they knew, was an arrogant force, a wild untamed, a power as unpredictable as the children who either turned to the trees for shelter and solace or carving and mauling. How could the wind bend with the grace of a blade of wheat? How could a sparrow lift his small self

up   up   **up**   up   up

when met by the gale of the wind? 'I can tell you,' said the smooth wandering stream. 'It is because in their differences they find their own lost pieces.'

The *aspie* parent. We bring a host of nuances to the act of parenting. Obviously, our presentation is, in many ways, very different from our neurotypical counterparts. Typical parents act, perceive, respond, communicate and guide their children in manners not ordinary to the aspie. At bottom, each kind of parent wants the same kinds of things for their children –

happiness, success, and good health – but at our top, we reach for those goals by climbing on different sorts of branches.

I worry my children wish they had a mom who was more like other moms. I worry they wish they had a normie mom. Sure, life is what you are used to, but perceptions can be changed by what you see. I asked my girls and my husband to list the various ways I am a, well, not quite normal mom. Here, in no particular order, is their top ten list.

1. You do embarrassing things in public.

2. You talk to yourself in public. Loudly!

3. You cannot stand smells and noises.

4. You just act weird.

5. You do not like going to my events.

6. You talk big with your hands, using some sort of weird sign language.

7. You interrupt people when they are talking.

8. You focus too much on little things.

9. You are not fun at the mall.

10. You go on and on and on about the same stuff even over and over and over.

On the surface, it seems these are generic kinds of complaints, the kind that any child or any spouse would level against anyone. Maybe they are. The difference lies not in what the complaint is, but rather, why it is offered. For example, neurotypical parents will surely embarrass their kids for one reason or another. They will no doubt talk to themselves on occasion, object to their child's loud music and smelly rooms, and act weird just by virtue of the fact that they are acting like a parent. But, will they go as far as the aspie parent might go? Will they walk over to their child's teacher with the full intention of reaching their fingers into her mouth to remove a chunk of spinach from her teeth? I doubt it. But I would. I did. Did it embarrass my child? You bet. Did it embarrass the teacher? Luckily, no. This teacher knows most of what there is to know about my AS and so was able quickly to determine I was about to go beyond the steps of the norm. Just as I came within reach of her mouth, she took two steps back, which gave me a bit of passing time to tell her, rather than show her, she had a piece of spinach in her mouth. My daughter, realizing I was poised to put my paw right into the teacher's mouth, jumped from her chair, grabbed me by the arm, spun me around to face her and whispered in her loudest whisper, 'Mom! You are embarrassing me! Stop it!' And with that, she trotted back to her seat all smiles, as if nothing out of the ordinary had passed our way. 'Oops,' I said to the teacher as she smiled a big spinach-less grin. 'Oops,' she laughed in return. You see, aspie parents can be extra good at embarrassing their kids.

NT parents are not perfect either. They are fraught with frailties and self-absorbing causes and the stuffings that go with adulthood. They will miss their children's piano recitals, their goal scoring games, their puppet shows and their field trips. But why will they miss them? I asked my husband that very question and he responded by saying, 'There are plenty of reasons. The parent might have unfinished work to tend to, a meeting with someone, a headache, a busy schedule of his own or he might just be too tired.' Regular reasons. NT reasons that are of a different sort when compared to aspie reasons.

Shortly after we moved to our new state, my almost aspie daughter enthusiastically told me about her latest opportunity to join yet another new organization. About the time the dinner dishes needed to be cleared from the table, this child came to me with a flyer announcing it was time to join the Girl Scouts. As I read the flyer, I felt my needs separate from my wants. I wanted so very much to share my daughter's enthusiasm. I wanted to shout Yahoo and laugh about all the fun we would surely share in the Girl Scouts club. But I couldn't. My mouth dried and my head started to pound as I pictured the filling Girl Scouts is made from. Social parties filled with nuances and expectations I would not see...sharing small spaces with strangers on camping trips...loud and active little girls...interpersonal communications with other moms...car pooling with people I had never met...phone calls from other moms asking me to volunteer for things I had no experience of...new faces I wouldn't recognize and new names I would forget...these are the very kinds of things that make life hard for me, even now that I'm on the residual end of my AS. My needs told me I couldn't do this. Not now. Not after we had just moved to the area. Not now, not when my routines were so new and foreign. Not today. I was still shaky in my own skin, itchy when I tried to go into town. I was knee wobbly and anxious to begin with. Joining a new club when I was barely keeping my head above water, well — that spelled nothing but disaster to me. I had learned from a hard set of experiences that I cannot take on too many new things at once. I simply did not have the energy to take on Girl Scouts; worse yet, I didn't have the confidence.

It is hard to lift my head when I realize seemingly uncomplicated things stare me down and make me weak. In the old days, way before I knew about antidepressant medications and bio-feedback and cognitive therapy, I would have hit the wall of depression over my inability to be like other moms. I would have chastised myself for making such a big deal over something so small as Girl Scouts. I would have condemned myself for not having the kinds of natural instincts I needed to walk into a meeting of moms with confidence and fun ideas to share. I would have hated myself.

These days I accept the fact that NT everyday things will remain a challenge for me. A challenge, not a brick wall. These days, I allow myself a day or two to stew in the newness of the thing that is facing me. I sit with it, ponder it, work it over in my mind. I picture what kinds of things the activity will demand of me. I picture where it will take me, the things I will do, the potential enjoyment I could find. I block out my imagination so it doesn't take hold and encourage my thoughts to grow grey. I tell myself, 'Don't go there', don't wander into the darkness of depression and the shakes of anxiety, despite the temptation. I force myself to compare the new event with something similar I've successfully enjoyed in the past and then I set about convincing myself this time will be no different. I acknowledge there will be a period of discomfort, times when I will want to crawl under my bed and moments when I think I'll scream from the strain of trying too hard to fit in too quickly. But, I tell myself, this time will pass. Eventually, somehow, some way, I will find my way through the mess and to the spot where I can actually look forward to the activity.

When my daughter told me she wanted to be a Girl Scout, I was scared and uncertain about my abilities to help her become one, but I was motivated at least to try. Three months after she had joined, I looked back and saw I was not frightened any more, despite the mess-ups along the way. It no longer mattered that I had frequently misunderstood directions to events, or lost track of the days I was to volunteer. I had all but forgotten my nerves directed my impulses until my thoughts came out confused and my voice too fast and too loud. I was able to shrug off the fact that when the journey first began, I routinely went home in a lather of sweat and a stream of frustration tears. Looking back, I am thrilled I persevered. I wouldn't now be a semi-normal Girl Scout mom if I hadn't. I would have missed so much.

I wish life were easier for me to learn. I don't understand why I hit every new event as if it was my first day on earth, but so it goes. I am an aspie and aspies have to crawl when they are on un-familiar ground. The good news for most of us – when we are motivated or interested enough, we can usually find a way to make it to where we want to go…some way, somehow.

Many is the time I try to hide my apprehensions and my inability to cope from my children, but the older my children get, the more savvy they become in figuring out when my AS keeps me from doing the everyday, regular kinds of things their friends' moms do. My oldest daughter is particularly good at seeing through me. I call her my 'dress rehearsal' child. She was the daughter I built my can and cannot perimeter around. This child keeps me intact. She gives me the strength to explore and placate my needs no matter when, no matter what, no matter where. What a gift to me who so often wanders too near the line I should not cross.

When someone cares enough to let me be who I need to be, several things happen. On the one hand, this concern nudges me to give in to the need to touch the world in a way that makes sense to me. This is essential for my nerves and my learning process. When I relate to things on my level first, I can then, and only then, extrapolate what I need in order to move the understanding on to an NT's take on the matter. In other words, I have to know what I'm dealing with before I can figure out how to translate that situation or those thoughts into NT talk. It behoves me to explore things through my aspie eyes first. This usually means I will come at something full force. If I'm involved with an academic class I will ask the teacher a myriad of questions from the basic to the advanced, until I have exhausted as many thoughts as I can muster. I will look up experts on the subject and write them letters via the Internet, asking them, too, for their thoughts. I will turn to every book and every article I can lay my hands on, all to gather everything I can on the subject. I cannot pretend to understand everything I gather and discover, I simply remain addicted to the search process. Once I begin exploring something, I cannot seem to let it go until I've saturated myself in it. Sometimes the saturation process is quicker than others. I might feel full after a day of research. I might still be hungry after a year spent on the subject. It all depends on how deeply rooted the material is and on how quickly I am able to understand it.

Academic things come to me far faster than life things. I think that is because academic things, with the exception of opinion papers and other things philosophical, are less layered than life. So when I am out and about exploring the world as it comes to me in the form of people, I scramble to gather information, fast and furiously. Sometimes this works just fine. Other times, I try too hard to know too much about too many too quickly. I reckon I don't have the luxury to sit back and ponder. I always assume I have to be quick on my feet and fast to come to a clear understanding of the whos or whats that are facing me. I end up tipping into overload. My oldest daughter tends to notice the moment I do.

Every school year, I take my daughters to the mall to buy new school clothes. I try to take them one at a time because it is easier to focus my attention and remain calm, when I am only having to deal with one person at a time. I usually take my oldest first because she helps me fit into the mall scene so that by the time I take my other girls, I have a bit of recent experience to relate to, and so, a bit of knowledge to keep me guided. For example, my oldest will script me through the mall telling me to relax, take deep breaths, concentrate on having fun. She will steer me from overwhelming stores and help me figure out the map of the mall so I don't wander aimlessly for hours on end. She'll prompt me to remember where our car is parked in relationship to the stores we visit, so that the next time I come, I can park in the same area and so not lose the car when I come back with her little sisters. Normally, my oldest and I have a relatively safe and sound time at the malls. With her help, I can fit in pretty near the normal…unless something really wild comes at us. Last year's shopping spree came at us with its teeth bared.

When we first got to the mall, all seemed almost perfect. I was relatively comfortable on this day and happily geared up for a good time with my daughter. The mall was calm by most mall standards. There were no busy patterns jumping at my eyes, no busy crowds pushing against me. Nothing blared out, nothing shook my bones, nothing pinched my nerves. So far, so good, I thought. We went from store to store looking for bargains and my daughter's version of style, just like any other mom and daughter team would do. Then, the tides turned. As bad luck would have it, my daughter's favorite clothes were sold in a store that was obviously managed by a very NT crowd. The moment we stood in front of the shop, I threw my hands to my ears and let go with a 'What's that noise? Who can stand this noise?' screech that continued and continued even after people started to stare. Music blared from the public address system loudly enough to curdle blood. Within a few minutes, my daughter took my arm and told me in no uncertain terms, 'We are leaving this place right now.' Chagrined, I implored her to stay until she found the outfit she had wanted.

'I'm so sorry,' I stammered. 'Please stay until you find what you like. I'll wait outside.'

'No,' came the reply, 'We are out of here.'

At that moment I would have given this child my charge card with my permission to max it out, but she would have none of it.

We went home without her favorite brand of clothes. I knew I had blown it, but I did not know how to make it right. Later that night, my daughter came to me with an essay she had written for school. It was an attack on the same store that had nearly taken me away from my daughter's trust and respect. In the essay, my daughter spelled out, in no uncertain terms, that the policy of blasting the airwaves with loud music was an insult to many who suffered from auditory dysfunction problems, and that further, the decibel levels of their music must have surely had a detrimental effect on their youngest customers and the employees for whom there was no escape.

My oldest daughter rescued her aspie mother from sure pain that day. She kept herself cool and she gave me dignity. She could have ranted and raved and shouted, 'I hate you.' But she did not. She saw, when no one else likely did, that I was reacting to sensory overload and the bombs it can explode within me. She knew without being told that it was an aspie thing keeping me from doing an everyday mom and daughter thing. But she paid that no attention. She showed her concern for me, no matter. From this daughter, I learned a lesson I hope other aspie families memorize – prioritize. Put the important stuff first; when it guides you, all will not be lost.

Asperger Syndrome does not always peek over the top. It is not always obvious even to the people who know us well. Not, at least, when the person affected is at the high-functioning end of the syndrome. Debate whirls as to whether we on the high end are aspie enough to qualify for services or even sympathy. I wish those who doubt our needs could perch themselves on my thought waves for just one day. Perhaps then they could touch the reality that occurs for many of us who have learned how to fake it by emulating others, keeping our confusion a secret, covering up our perseverations and interests, avoiding social gatherings and team meetings at all cost, applying our intellect to emotional jams... Would those who dismiss us understand our quandary better if they could feel the stress and worry we carry in our bellies for fear our true personas will sneak out and scare away the few real friends we have and all the hope for success we hold? Adults with AS know full well that Asperger Syndrome can be sneaky and coy, or loud and forthright. We know some of us are dripping in it and others of us are sprinkled by it. But no matter what, we know we are a community, no matter how the AS presents in us.

I tend to be a sprinkled variety aspie. When I am not making public behavior slips, you can bet my aspie traits are simply manifesting in some other, albeit possibly quite subtle way. But even subtle differences can nick, especially when the difference keeps me from relating to my children. When I cannot find the impetus to play the games my children turn to for fun simply because I have become too mired in my own obsessions, I bruise my children. When my inability to get hold of abstract concepts and the main idea keep me from helping the girls with their homework, I let them down. When I cannot help them organize their belongings for my own executive functioning skills are too weak, I confuse them. And when I cannot help the girls figure out a new dance craze because my bilateral coordination problems trip me even now that I am an adult, I keep them from smiling.

These are bite-sized things to us adults, but to children they can stand out as the most important events life has to offer. If the aspie parent fails at the small stuff time after time after time, what happens when the big stuff smashes itself against the wall? What then? What happens to my relationship with my girls when I have to tell them I cannot for the life of me understand their personal communication problems, the kinds of he said, she said, what do I say, things that are as foreign to me as Latin is to my girls. How can I explain to them their mom doesn't think like lots of people do, that she finds it hard to figure out what the body means when the mouth is silent, that she gets caught up in background noise when someone is talking to her, that gossip and small talk are mostly meaningless to her because they deal with emotions and hearsay situations that ring no common bell with mom. What can I offer as an excuse when they see me walking through the halls of their school in my pajamas, happily on my way to bringing them a book they forgot in the car? Will they believe me when I tell them I'm not playing some kind of embarrass-the-kids game? Will they understand when I tell them their perceptions of acceptable and non-acceptable are shades different from mine?

I pray so. I think so. But to be sure, I try extremely hard to pull out each and every one of my strengths when I am with my girls. Not strengths like NTs have. Aspie strengths are cured by the syndrome that steeps us in aspie tea, the result of which is an intense and complex flavor. If NTs are black tea, we aspies are a complex blend of herbs and spices. One is not preferable over the other, both are simply different in their expressions and different on the palate. My strengths come from those intensities we aspies are naturally wired to. For example, think about the effects a super strong sensory system – a solid aspie trait – can have on the rearing of kids. I can smell my children's skin and hair and breath to know if illness is on its way to their body far before a fever confirms the fact. I wake to their night whimpers despite my ear plugs, my own deep dreams, and the fact that my room sits on a floor far away from theirs. I can feel the twitches and shivers in their bellies and in their lungs and in their movements, long before the asthma attack or the allergies or the stomach flu make their presence known. I am like a service dog first trained to rely on her nose, eyes and ears. Like that dog, my natural instincts are quite basic. But, oh, so powerful.

Power. It yields strength. I am an awesomely focused mom, as strong in my ability to fixate tenaciously on my children's tiniest details as I am in my ability to stand up for my children's individuality. While many see my tremendous attention to my children's lives as proof of my being overprotective and paranoid, I disagree. I think my ability to hone in on the teeniest aspect of my children's character and physical being is an excellent mothering skill. I analyze my children's strengths and weaknesses by the minute. I am the parent who is never surprised at teacher parent conferences. I am the parent who can instantly recall, catalog and compare their personal accomplishments, from the way they tie a shoe, to the way they cross a T, to the way they circle the dots on an answer sheet. I am the kind of mom who creates detailed lists of the kinds of things that upset or console her kids, the kinds of things that turn them into kind humans or angry children, and the subjects that bring them joy or pain. And while I cannot readily or easily tell why they are upset, I can see, from the changes in their eye focus and their body stance, that they are upset. It doesn't matter much that I have to ask my kids directly what is bothering them, so long as they are prepared to tell me when I ask. Ah, but these are the very kinds of thing NT parents can do. Yes, if they seriously and con-scientiously put the most powerful part of their mind to it. I don't have to put anything to the act, I just do it. Attention to detail is a natural to an aspie. In fact, I am so good at noticing tiny nuances, tiny changes in behavior, tiny deviations from the norm, that my friends routinely ask my advice about matters they worry they will miss regarding their own children.

As difficult as it is for me to interpret NT behaviors when I am on the outside looking in, I have learned that, provided I have enough time, I can usually get to the bottom of the pile when I am trying to figure someone out. Simply put, I analyze my way through people. I look at them as intricate problems that need to be solved. I put them under microscopes and take note of the things they do with their hands, their eyes, their legs, their entire body. I listen to their voices for changes in their pitch and tone and cadence. I compare how they are acting to how they have acted under different conditions. I can tell when they are lying by noting changes in these behaviors, even though I won't know why they are lying. I realize full well that my direct approach to people solving is somewhat disconcerting to others. But I also know it typically gets good results.

I think I disarm people with my ability to remain objective and detached. It must be hard, I reason, for others to relate to me when I come across so raw and open. I think I unnerve people, particularly if I somehow catch them off guard. I have heard it said that I am too confrontational, too pushy and too arrogant. I don't mean to be. I don't literally push or shove anyone, I don't get into arguments unless debating the truth or fairness of an idea is considered an argument. Nor do I think I am better than anyone else. Far from it. I don't have any idea why so many NT people find me unsettling, but a good friend of mine thinks she does know. 'Apparently,' this friend told me, 'NTs find you aspie types too unpredictable and too likely to point out when they themselves have made a mistake.' Odd, but that is exactly what I would say about most NTs.

Within our family, at least, we aspies can hopefully be who we need and want to be. Though this is helpful for us on an individual basis, it is not all that easy for us as a whole. The mix of our AS traits and our NT traits tends toward the lumpy rather than the smooth. Of course this creates many problems for all of us. Mostly it causes dents in our self-esteem and in our sense of security. When they get to big and bad, my emotions swell up until I am eventually stripped of my logic. I rely on my logic. It makes sense. I am uncomfortable in the arms of emotions. NTs might argue emotion is the key to understanding, that through the heart comes empathy. I would disagree. In my terms, emotions are too vulnerable. They can easily get muddled and colored by everyone's perspective and other people's agendas. They can easily undo me. When I am logical, I find there is much in my children I can tolerate, much I am able to fathom, and much I am able to help them through. But when I am emotional, the logic disappears and then I am left too high strung and too demanding. Only my intellect, so it seems, can guide me to the end of my problems.

My aspieness makes me a different mom. Not a better or a worse mom, but a different mom. I am still a mom that cares and loves and worries and watches and helps and does for her children. I am also a mom who might need some explaining now and then.

'Why do you insist on telling the girls about your problems?' a well-meaning friend once said to me. I have given that sentiment a great deal of thought. I have heard counselors and analysts and physicians and neighbors say that kids do not need to know one thing about their parents' past, that they don't need to know their parents' motives or rationale, that 'Because I said so' is good enough for anyone under the age of emancipation. Thing is, I do not say things like regular parents do. Nor do I do things like regular parents do. I strongly believe that if my girls do not know the secrets behind their mom, they will be caught in my wave. They need to know their mom has unconventional

ways of saying and doing things, or they are likely to get too dis-
tracted by my methods and too far away from my message. I
believe I would be a forever-lost enigma if I did not help my
daughters explore life through my eyes. Without a guidebook of
me, how could I expect my people to figure me out? How could
I expect them to appreciate me? But more important, how could
I hope to understand them? If I didn't tell them when I'm
confused by the little things they've said, show them when I'm
overwhelmed by stuff they take for granted, and listen when
they tell me I've lost them along the way, we would lose one
another.

Self-analysis does not come easy to the aspie, particularly the
male aspie. Some of us never get to the point where we can look
inward and explain outward. I am very lucky I can examine who
I am. I am even luckier I can share that knowledge with others.
This doesn't erase the fact that it is hard for me to disclose the
fact that I am not perfect and it does not ease my mind when I
worry I've disclosed too much. But my relationship with my
girls has proven there is strength in honesty and trust in truth.
Rather than being a burden to these young women, I believe I
am a role model for self-acceptance and self-discovery and
realism, but also a mom who is far from perfect, far from typical
and far from the model moms of fairy tales and nursery rhythms.
I think that is okay.

6

Speak Now or Forever Hold Your Peace

✎

Aspie Wedding Vows

To my mate. Thanks for taking me on. I am not much for emotion as you know, but I want to tell you I think you are a nice person. I will not be telling you that too often because I just did and there really is no reason to repeat myself. I think our marriage will be an asset to us both. I promise to let you find your own space, breathe your own air and make your own goals. I promise I will not ask you to change who you are and I ask you to let me stay who I am. I promise I will be a dependable, loyal, stable and honest partner. I promise to love you for better or for worse; even if I do not show it, it will be so. When I move about the world without you, do not think it means I have lost my affection for you. When I turn my attention to my obsessions, do not think it means I have forgotten you. When I forget to mention you look lovely, do not think it is not so. I would not have joined you in marriage if I did not love you and want you in my life.

In my first book, *Pretending to be Normal: Living With Asperger's Syndrome*, there is an entire chapter devoted to the relationship my husband and I have managed to build after fifteen years together. Bookends, I called us, two people who support one another so that the stuff in between does not make us crumble. Since publishing that book, countless people have asked how our marriage comes so easy to us. At least I think that is what they ask. Their words can be somewhat more jagged: 'How do you put up with her?' NTs ask my husband. 'How do you make him leave you be?' aspies ask me. I admit to being hopelessly aspie regarding this marriage dilemma. Frankly, I did not know one existed. Neither did my husband. Perhaps he is more aspie than we realize. Thanks to the help of some dear NT friends, I have since been re-educated. With honesty and objectivity, these friends shared with me their marriage woes, sorrows, wishes and hopes. I used their thoughts to paint this chapter. I hope I understood them clearly...

Less than two hours after my husband and I were married, he cried a river. 'Why is Tom crying?' I asked no one in particular. 'He's probably sad he got married,' said someone who knew Tom well. For a very long time, I thought that answer was said in honesty. I never suspected 'he's crying because he married you' could be a joke or a tease. How could anything hurtful be meant as a tease? That makes no sense. At least not to me. But then, I am an aspie. A dozen years passed before I learned my Tom cried because the outpouring of affection we received on our wedding day overwhelmed him. It never dawned on me Tom's tears were okay tears. I did not know tears of the very wet kind could be happy tears. A droplet here or there – maybe that could be a show of happiness. But a waterfall? Had to be grief. Big grief. Imagine how it felt to think my wedding day was a sad day for the man I decided to spend the rest of my life with. Not a big boost to the self-esteem, but more importantly, not a very big boost to the level of trust aspies need in order to grow and progress.

Aspies and neurotypicals. By our nature, we are in many ways unconnected, different, poles apart. Sometimes I think it a marvel anything one says to the other ever makes more than a modicum of sense. Those who suggest we are peoples from two separate cultures are correct by my estimation. But is it impossible for people from different parts of the world to ignite a union? Of course not. It is just a bit harder.

In and of itself, marriage is a boulder that needs to be gently chipped at, tumbled and polished, if it is to show the gem at its core. Particularly for aspies. Any relationship that is dependent upon the outpouring of emotion, an understanding of others' perspectives and intentions, deeply embedded social rules and traditions, and the superimposing of interests with needs is, by definition, a relationship that will play hard to aspie crowds. It pains me to hear NTs talk about the discontent they feel in their marriage. I want to tell them to take a big breath, to act like a duck and let the water roll off their back more. I want to take them by the arm and bring them to a place where the past sits before them clearly and objectively, happy and warm. A time when things made a different kind of sense. A time when that which looks so foreign now, made all the sense in the world. *'Find your first days together,'* I would say. *'Sneak back in time to the moment you met your aspie. What did you see in him then? What did you love and adore? What was it about his walk and his talk and his smile and his frown that made you fall in love with him? Was it his dependability? His honesty? His sense of responsibility? Did he make you feel safe? Did he make you feel smart? Was he a friend no matter what, no matter when? Did he answer when you called? Did he thrill you by wanting to spend all his time with you and no one else? Were his quirks endearing to you, his differences intriguing? Did you grow strong when you sheltered him from a world he saw as hard? And then I would whisper in their ear, Did you think your mate would change after you married him? Did you think you had the right to want him to?'*

Whispers. Nudges. Small steps. Baby steps. None of us can run to face the reality of a marriage that has not become what we dreamed it would. We have to get to that summit after we have lost our breath, scraped our knees, burned our skin and nearly given up the journey. It is hard to stare straight at the life that caught you when you were not looking. It can make a person feel trapped and scared. It is better if the whisper holds your hand while you peek at what you see. One by one, the rocks will give way and one by one, new bulbs will grow. One by one...

My friends tell me they are hurt by their aspie's lack of affection. They tell me they are lonely too often, misunderstood too frequently, and left out in the cold on too many nights. I recognize why they would feel each of these emotions. I empathize, but I do not relate. From my frame of mind, it is not necessary to hear I am loved each and every day. It is not important for me to be cherished like a glass bubble. It is not in me to feel lonely when I am alone. But it is in me to sense others have needs I do not share. If my husband were to tell me he felt sad and lonely when I was working on my computer all night long, I would respond by asking him, 'Why?' or 'That's interesting.' It would not come to me he was trying to tell me he wished I would turn the computer off and spend time with him. No, he would have to tell me directly he needed or wanted my devoted attention. Telling me he was lonely when I worked, would not register, 'I need you to be with me.' If my husband were to ask me if I thought he looked handsome, I would reply honestly either way. I would not fathom he was really, secretly, wanting me to tell him I found him attractive. I would take his question at face value and answer if I thought he looked handsome or not handsome. I would think he wanted a true and straightforward answer to his question. I would not have added superficial layers to his question nor would I have guessed he wanted something he did not directly request. My responses would not have come from being heartless or uncaring. I would not have intentionally ignored the desire of his heart. I would never intentionally hurt any person I care about. I do not think any decent person would.

The lack of physical affection also upsets the NT frame of mind. Apparently, this is a need very basic to their sense of self and their marital security. NTs enjoy touch and physical closeness, because they receive both emotional and physical pleasure from it. Many aspies do not. Sensory issues can plague our ability to touch. Fingers knotted through fingers for handholding are like logs jamming their way through a tight fist. Massages feel like hot bricks beating against open sores. Tickles become like beetle bugs caught between your clothing and your skin. Sensory issues can make physical affection extremely challenging for the aspie. They can make closeness next to impossible. As difficult as life without touch might be for the NT, life with touch can be just as difficult for the aspie. Together, each must work to find a compromise that will harm no one. Tom and I have worked out a simple plan. He shows me through his actions if he wants me to hold his hand or sit beside him or give him an embrace. I tell him through my voice if I can or cannot oblige. He knows better than to get his feelings hurt by my rebuffing. He knows I would warm up to him, if I could. He knows I will when I can. On the days when my sensory system is more quiet than normal, I will certainly approach him and supply him with an unexpected bit of affection. I know, without even being told, he will always welcome my attention. He has learned to turn to our children for a hug if I am vacant. He has learned to modify his needs. And I have learned to strengthen my ability to touch more often than I used to. Slowly and patiently, we have met in the middle.

In a perfect world, everyone would know most everything he needed to know about his partner long before he agreed to become a couple. From knowledge comes a schema that will be able to build safe roads between the predictable and the unforeseen. Without a solid schema, everyone involved is likely to stumble into ruts. Each stumble will swell the ruts deeper until chasms are made. NTs will eventually learn, from trial and error, how to climb beyond or around those customs. Aspies will need more than trial and error. They will need direct instruction. Trials and tribulations will not become lessons learned, they will simply be memories that stand on their own with little relationship to anything other than the day they occurred. If NTs knew this about their aspies, if they were accurately aware of all the major strengths and limitations of their partner, they would be better prepared to handle the controversial situations that will be bound to find them. But the world is anything but a perfect place. Odd flashes of light can draw people together for nameless reasons. Situations draw us in; events pull us together, no matter, sometimes, the sphere from which we spin.

I have heard countless NTs claim their aspie mates are cruel and mean spirited, too hard headed and undisciplined. And while I will admit we may appear to be all of those things, we are not, in our spirit. We do not wake up in the morning goal setting to kill another good day for our NT mates. We do not plan to aggravate or annoy. Truth be told, we easily come to feel as if we are the persecuted, the party who has been misunderstood. I wonder, as I hear the vocal NTs express their marital concerns, if they realize a room full of married aspies would have a great number of complaints to levy, too. Surely, NTs do not think we are able to ignore being told how hard we are to live with, how insensitive we are and how miserable we make others. The issue of mutual communication runs both ways. NTs cannot understand our ways and we cannot understand theirs. Perhaps it is as my aspie father says, 'The neurotypicals have a better press agent than we do.' But then again, they also have more tender hearts. As vulnerable as aspies can be, we by and large can survive greater damage to the inside than NTs can. That is the good news which comes from being hard crusted. The bad news is, we can be harder to fix once we have been broken. NTs and aspies both need tune-ups. They both need protection from pain.

KEEPING THE HURT FROM LASTING

○ Be realistic about your expectations. Very realistic. For example, keep in mind it is rare for a person to be shiny on both sides of the coin. If he weathers the world as a stoic and logical thinker, he will not be a romantic who surprises you with fantasy-filled trips. You have to decide which traits you value most and you need to be willing to forgo looking for the mirror traits within the same person.

○ Create your own kind of marriage. Try to relinquish the traditional roles and invent new ones that are better suited to you and your aspie. My parents, for example, have had separate homes for most of their married life. They each have their own totally independent identities, their own friendship circles and their own interests. Their relationship centers on joint business ventures, intellectual pursuits and their shared admiration of their grandchildren. They have come to believe and understand a partner does not need to fill every void in the heart.

○ Build your own world. Find fresh ways to enjoy the things you need, but your aspie does without. Find a friend to socialize with. Take an extra-curricular class with a neighbor. Get a pet, work with children, or volunteer at a nursing home if you need lots of physical attention.

○ Find new ways to help one another show your love and support. My father brings my mother peonies from his garden as a way to show his affection. Words are not necessary to him. Fresh picked peonies he grew himself, go farther in expressing his care than a sentence would. My husband and I are also action over words people, even if the actions are subtle and simple. Long ago, my husband told me 'I show you I love you, I don't have to tell you all the time.' He is right. Every morning he makes my coffee. That is a sign of his affection. Every day I make him laugh. That is a sign of my affection. Every Sunday for as long as we have lived together, we have watched the same morning magazine show together. That is our sign of the contentment we share. We could expect more, but why would we? We have found little things can make life just as nice and pretty as big chunks of words or hugs, maybe even more so.

o Set aside a private area in your home or yard which will symbolically hold your frustrations away from your day-to-days. This is the spot you will go to when you need to blow off some steam or cry over a forgotten anniversary. Put a few items that remind you of the frustrations you feel, for they do need validation in some form, and a few items that remind you of your spouse's concern for you. Sometimes a visual and tactile reminder of things positive and not so positive can sit side by side in harmony, a lesson worth bringing home to the heart.

o Through it all, keep your self-worth in tow. Come to terms with the fact that the aspie is not on a course to ride you into the ground. If the aspie shows a lack of emotion, a reluctance to show much affection, a hesitation to spread compliments like butter, and an inability to be a traditional romantic, do not assume this has everything to do with you. It may in fact, have nothing to do with you. Remember that aspies do not normally find these kinds of attributes essential to their core. Try to bring objectivity and balance to your worries.

Aspies may do a very good job of giving their partner every ounce of love they have. The trouble comes when *what they have* falls short of what the NT partner needs. This problem quickly goes beyond the scope of coupled NT relationships. Aspies miss the opportunities that spell out what their partner needs and desires. We tend to respond from our own center of being. Some call us egocentric. I object to that word. I prefer to call us self-contained. We are our own boutique, our own small shop that puts everything we need on a display shelf only we can see. If the things others need are not on our shelves, we simply do not see them. Then again, if new things are put on our shelves, we might not choose to pick them up. We may stay tucked within our own world's expectations and needs no matter how pretty the NT sparklies are. We might refuse new things, no matter what. In short, we might present to the NT world as rigid and glued.

Why will she never admit when she is wrong? Do we have to do everything her way? Does he really think the world is either black or white? Typical questions from typical NTs. My typical answers: Because she is not wired to be flexible, yes and yes. Like a bed fixed for a drill sergeant, when our minds are made up, they are set good and solid with tight military corners and coin bouncing straightness. There is no inclination, no impulse, and no reason known to us, to go back and ruffle the covers. The bed is tidy and firm. Why in the world would we go back and mess it up?

Think of the aspie as one who can walk the skinniest balance beam without falling off. We have a linear line to think about, act upon and live for. Life goes this way or that way, not this *and* that way. Rules are meant to be followed. Right is right. Wrong is unacceptable. Schedules are made to be followed, they keep things safe and neat and tidy. Surprises and spontaneity are as unwelcome as rain at a picnic. We do not like things to alter from their predicted route. But this is more than a personal preference. The tendency to be rigid and unbending, rule-oriented and scheduled, is an aspie hallmark. While we sit persistent, NTs walk with cognitive pliability. NTs are more wont to engage in behaviors that stretch even their elasticity to its limits. The aspie finds it hard to go beyond his comfort zone and harder still to fix a cognitive mess. We get lost when we try to find our way back through the weeds of our mistakes. Getting lost makes us nervous and edgy. It can make us cranky and even hostile. NT attempts to crack our concrete come to us through sentiments like 'How could you say such a thing? Did you not know you hurt my feelings? What makes you think I want to hear that coming from you? Don't you ever listen to me? You don't care what I think.' But these words do little to melt us. They become drums drowning out the tiny voice in the aspie heart that tries so desperately to reach the mind. Neurotypicals do not have tiny voices. They have strong, clear, multi-lingual voices that can be heard above the roar of the entire jungle. They are fully aware from the get-go that their partnership will require eons of rides on the merry-go-round of talk. They know there will be late nights of turbulent conversation, long stretches that make them feel like they are wearing a heavy sweater on a muggy morning, bumpy walks and brown fields. But these voices come to us as weeds stealing around our ankles until we are tripped and fallen. Because NTs expect their marriage course to need patching up now and then, they learn to prepare for those repairs and they learn to avoid the weeds. We aspies do not readily recognize trial and error will teach us new tricks. We are not programmed to think our marriage will need constant pruning and refurbishing. That mindset requires a cognitive flexibility we typically lack. It is a reference point that eludes us.

Failure to admit when we are wrong falls into the inflexible range, too. It necessitates the same problem-solving hierarchy that underscores any change in attitude or behavior – the hierarchy we are not wired to turn to. The aspie mindset and behavior patterns are set on an uphill course. We plod along, steadily and diligently, chugging up the rugged terrain with all our might so that turning back and re-focusing our energies would spell a certain wreck. We cannot simply turn about in mid-climb; we would tumble and crash. We have to finish our course until we reach the top of our destination and then, perhaps, if we are given the right food for thought, we will be able slowly to turn our mammoth sized engine in a new direction. Perhaps. Perhaps not. All will depend on the intervention we are given. Neither demands, nor pleas, will turn us around.

Casting blame to the wind, there are some practical strategies both groups can make use of to ease the communication pain. They are similar to the kinds of things marriage counselors would recommend to a totally NT union, with one important difference: aspie counseling needs to focus on cognitive analysis, not emotional analysis. The emotional train is a bumpy one for aspies. While we can learn to read nonverbal emotional cues and understand what emotions are and what they do, it is far easier (and far more natural) for us to work from the cognitive to the emotional, rather than from the emotional to the cognitive. Hence, when working on something as emotionally charged as a marriage in stress, I would humbly suggest the aspie's side of counseling should center on intellectual discussions and intellectual re-programming. Cognitive re-structuring will ultimately give us our best chance of re-figuring where we need to go and how we need to think.

RE-FOCUSING THE ASPIE

○ Speak logic not emotion. Yes, aspies have genuine feelings, but these feelings relate to reason better than the heart. Do not use words like 'always' or 'never' for we will take them very literally and get caught up in defending the fact that we are 'never always' doing this or that.

○ Do not bring up more than one issue at a time for discussion. If you try to address everything but the kitchen sink in your debate, the aspie will very quickly spiral into a mental free-fall. You may realize one issue has bearing on another, but the aspie may not. Deal with things one by one over a period of time.

o Make sure your verbals and nonverbals match. If you are angry, do not smile. This will only confuse the issue. If you are sad, do not scream as if you are angry. Stay basic. Sad = tears. Happy = smiles.

o Do not waste your time being sarcastic. The aspie will not catch the tone in your voice and will totally miss your point. Be direct and straightforward in your comments. The fewer the layers of meaning, the better.

o Write or draw your way through the discussion. It might be easier for the aspie to focus her thoughts if they are visual and not verbal. But remember the same rules apply for symbolic thought – no over generalizing or sarcasm is allowed.

o Try to use metaphors to make your point. Draw pictures with your words that help the aspie 'see' what you are trying to say.

o Avoid close proximity when you are discussing big issues. Close proximity includes riveting eye contact, touch, and short personal space. These behaviors can be very unsettling to an aspie, especially one in a state of flux.

o Establish a code word either one of you can use to signal you need a break. The moment the word is heard, the debate needs to come to a halt. Do not be surprised if you find the aspie uses the word more than he accepts it. It can be nearly impossible for the aspie to stop on a dime.

o If you suspect the aspie is totally unable to follow your line of reasoning, end the discussion as quickly as you can and let it rest. Do not return to the discussion until everyone has had ample time to rest his or her heart rate. Not only might this practice avoid the physical traumas that come from stress, it might also give the aspie the opportunity to unwind his weedy thoughts.

o Let the aspie know when she has understood you. Confirm it when she is on track and has made a point you needed to find. It is not fair to anyone if only negative comments are parlayed back and forth.

A stronger communication connection between the NT and the aspie will fix-up a fair share of partnership problems, but I fear one big issue will remain no matter how well the aspie and the NT have learned to understand and trust one another. Socializing. Just the idea of getting together with others I do not know very well is more than enough to send me into a frenzy. Party going is a spiky sport played in an arena filled with wrap-around passageways and mirrored rooms. Picking out what to wear, what to talk about, whom to talk to, how to quit talking to whomever, when to arrive, when to leave, what to bring, who to bring, where to stand, how to sit, what to eat, where to eat, how to eat, all compound the difficulty level of the game. Add upon these variables the problems that will surely show up in the way of non-verbal misunderstandings, aspie-led monologues about favorite perseverations, the inability to face read and the problems with mind reading, and woe becomes the aspie party-goer.

No matter how hard I try, I cannot find a way to enjoy myself at parties. I do, however, find many ways to fake it as if I am having the time of my life. My outside tells funny stories, smiles all the time, nods at everything she hears and stands put in the corner while my husband goes to get me the food he thinks I can handle without spilling all over myself. My inside weeps silent jitters that would race me out of the room if for just one moment I let them have their rein.

Most people have no idea my ability to socialize is so filled with flaws. I do an excellent job of covering up my apprehensions and my shortcomings. I know plenty of aspies who would say the same thing about themselves. In and of itself, this admission is not necessarily good, not if it means we are suffering in silence. On the other hand, it might well mean we are on our way towards mastery of the subject. The first step might indeed be superficial, but the continuing steps might well go beyond the surface and over to the real level of mastery. This leads me to think socializing is one trait of aspiehood that benefits from loads of practice, and conversely, a trait which will get more fixed if it is not practised. In my own experience, for example, it is far more difficult to get back into socializing rituals if I have avoided them for too long. I think the key might be a consistent drip of friendship gatherings rather than a few big splashes every year or so.

SOCIALIZING THE ASPIE WAY

o Keep party gatherings small. The guest list should be built around a few people the aspie knows well enough to enjoy being around.

o Set short time limits for your socializing. Stick to them. This small measure of predictability will go a long way toward calming the aspie.

o Practice socializing lingo and behaviors in the safety of the home. Go over every issue that may creep up. This could include everything from not talking with your mouth full to personal space reminders, to how to excuse oneself from a chat.

o Encourage the aspie to use favorite stories, which have been proven entertainment pieces. Conversely, encourage the aspie not to share stories which have any risk of being humiliating.

o Prompt the aspie to rely on an innocuous calming stim when they get too nervous in public. Some aspies I know chew gum, others rock or sway back and forth and still others rub a small tangible something in the palm of their hand. Along these lines, find a way to signal to the aspie should he come out with a stim at the gathering that would be potentially embarrassing for him.

○ Avoid gatherings that happen in places that would over-stimulate the aspie. In the long run, it really is better to beg off some dates than it is to try to master them all, no matter what.

All marriages go through ups and downs. Some make it whole throughout a lifetime; others bleed to death in infancy. The path the aspie/NT union takes will in large part depend on the NT's ability to be flexible and empathetic. It will also depend on the aspie's ability to grow and give to the NT who loves him. As with any union, the aspie/NT marriage will not work unless both partners work at it. The trick will be to discover non-traditional ways to communicate, live and enjoy one another.

7

Teeter Totter

I dream we are in a setting far from the real. Way back when, we would live. In a time when computers and telephones and radios and cars were yet to find their way into fantastical dreams. In our own ways, on our own terms, when we felt good and ready, we would do those things that bring us to happiness and well being. People, places, societies – their existence in our dailies would be gentle, nothing more than a thin sheet on a brilliantly cool evening. Our connection with one another would provide the fire that kept us warm, the fire that showed us who we really are. When people came to visit us, they would leave their preconceived notions regarding social acceptance and dress codes and trends and society's superficial bits and pieces at our doorway, much like visitors keep dirty shoes on the welcome mat. We would talk to our friends and visitors with earnest interest and real concern. Things like the weather, health, future goals and tomorrow's dreams, recollections of memories spent around tables of good meals and pretty horizons would cause us to remark. We would communicate through the universals – scientific discoveries, nature and her habits, music, art, drama and eating. We would not spend an inkling of time contemplating how we could trip up our guests with illogical debates or a convoluted game of guess what I'm thinking. No. Our time spent with others would be much

like the time we would spend with our own. It would be a time
based on the real important matters of living like honesty and
acceptance and respect. In my dreams...

Wonderful things can happen when aspies and NTs grow up
side by side. Each will learn more about life's angles than they
would have, had they grown up independent of one another. In
the comfort of a family, they can learn to appreciate individuality, to accept different points of view and the delicate practice of
patience. They can discover there are more than just a few ways
to see the world and plenty of definitions for the word 'ideal'.
And when all goes better than not, they can learn to make their
way through the muck of empathy and compassion, until they
reach the calm of tolerance and grace. What awesome opportunities the NT/AS mixed family can provide, if all goes well.

My only cause for alarm comes when I think of what sits on
the other end of these good things. It is the story of the fork in
the road – which way will my children go? Will they make it to
tolerance and grace or will they rage down the road where
anger, frustration, malice and put-downs rally? If Tom and I do
not work hard to steer the darkside from our family, we run the
risk of allowing one child to overshadow another. Such an
eclipse is unthinkable; however, there is no pretending AS and
NT children are cut from the same cloth. More to the point, there
is no solid reason to expect the two groups to behave as if they
are akin. This is not to suggest the two cannot mingle, rather it is
to point out the reality behind the differences between the two
groups. The differences come in tones. The tones tend to be
muted when the children are young, say under the age of six or
seven. They grow louder and stronger with each new candle on
the birthday cake. These differences catch kids by surprise. One
day, they are all innocents who share time and space as egocentric thinkers with simple needs and simple expectations. The
next day, lines are drawn, teams are established and cliques

gather those who walk their walk and talk their talk. The aspie stands alone.

I wanted more than anything in the world to be the fastest runner in my fifth grade class. I wasn't much of an athlete, unless I was running. I was fast, but not quite fast enough to beat a little girl named Michelle. She was the fastest on the playground. Fast kids were admired and looked up to. I liked being admired. It made me feel even faster. I practised and practised and ran and ran, but never could I beat Michelle. I came close, within a second or two, but I never crossed the finish line first. Then a miracle happened. Someone had invented a magic tennis shoe called 'P. F. Flyers'. All the ads said this shoe made you go so fast, you almost flew. I couldn't have been happier. P.F. Flyers would help me beat Michelle.

I remember the day my mother bought me the shoes. I held them in my hand with great reverence, almost fear. I hoped I could handle the speed they gave me. I hoped I didn't fly too far off the ground. Was I ready for such a big step in life? Such awesome power? After a day of looking at them and admiring them, I found what it took to put them on my feet. Look out, I warned myself, get ready to bolt like lightning. Wow, did I run fast. I was certain I ran near lift off. Now, I knew, I would be the fastest kid on the playground. I would be the best.

The next day we all lined up for our races. Michelle and I went last, as we always did. I was light on my feet and careful not to let the shoes do their magic until the race began. It was stressful trying to control their power, but I was motivated to win. At the sound of our teacher's whistle, Michelle and I took off on our fifty yard dash. I did not fly, I did not even go any faster. My shoes were not magic. Michelle won.

I was ten years old when I put on those shoes. How many ten-year-olds believe a shoe could make you Superman fast? My guess is, not many.

My P. F. Flyers did not teach me any lessons. They did not teach me my destiny was in my hands, nor did they even teach me I was far too literal a thinker. In my mind, the shoes had let me down, but I knew there were other miracles just around the bend that would bring me to some kind of great fortune. The next year, I found it in Wonder Bread. Wonder Bread sandwich bread made you tall. All their commercials said that. I loved tall people. I still do. I was a kid who grew into her height quickly. At eleven years old, I was five feet tall. That made me one of the tallest in my class. But not the tallest. I ached to be the best at something and since I was not the fastest, nor the best athlete, nor the smartest, nor anything else kids put a high price on, I decided I could at least be the tallest. I gave myself three months to make that goal come true. At the end of those three months, I would proudly march to the middle of the top row in our class picture. That was the spot reserved for the tallest student. I wanted it badly.

Wonder Bread became a favored play thing and my favorite food. I scrunched it up into little balls I could toss in my mouth like popcorn. I folded it this way and that until it looked like a fat fan. I tore it up into the kinds of little pieces you give to the birds, only I was the bird. I separated the crust from the soft white center, working hard to keep the crust in one square piece. I ate it plain most of the time, but sometimes I smeared it with peanut butter. I never toasted it. I liked it smooshy and fat.

Every day I measured myself. Every day I was confused. Why wasn't I getting taller? I had to be eating enough Wonder Bread. I was going through a loaf every day. What was the matter with me? Shoes didn't work on me and now bread wasn't working its magic either. A boy stands in the middle of my class picture. I never made it there. How come things never turned out like I thought they should? Why did miracles only happen to other kids?

I didn't come to understand the silliness behind my thinking until I formally studied propaganda in the sixth grade. I was loaded with embarrassment and a tattered ego during that unit of study. I ducked my head in shame when we got to the kinds of ads I had fallen prey to. I laughed along with my peers when they acknowledged how dumb someone would have to be to fall for such obvious deceptions. I went right along with the flow in talking about how only a little kid could believe what they heard and saw on TV. In my own mind, I chastised myself for being that dumb little kid who should have known better.

Direct teaching of advertising's deception saved me from taking television commercials so literally. I wish there had been some kind of teaching that would have taught me I was not a dumb little kid. Looking back, the only thing that would have made this kind of experience worse for me, would have occurred if I had shared my disappointment over my shoes or the bread with the kids on the playground. I can only imagine how they would have reacted to my stories. How many months of teasing would I have had to endure because I had taken the advertiser's sales pitch at the literal level? How many months of ridicule would I have faced if the other kids had known I REALLY thought my shoes would make me fast enough to leave the ground and my bread would REALLY make me the tallest kid in the picture?

Aspies typically know, on some level at least, that they are different from others. Maybe we can't quite put our finger on what those differences are, but we usually sense it. This knowledge can be very frightening, even if we are lucky enough to be a member of a tremendously supportive and caring family. There is a concern, very real and almost tangible, that warns us: if we admit we are different, we might be tricked into changing who we are. While we might agree to making compromises in our behaviors and while we might agree it is a good thing to work harder on communicating and understanding NT ways, it is quite another to consider throwing all of our being to the wind. After countless discussions with countless aspies of all sorts and abilities, I am of the opinion that for most of us, giving up all that we are is not only virtually impossible, but also incredibly unacceptable. I have met many aspies who tell me their family never did, and seemingly never will, accept their aspie traits. I have heard stories of abuse and neglect of aspie innocents that chill me to the bone. Even my worst nightmares keep me from picturing what it must feel like to be scorned by your family simply because you are different.

In this home, being different is the norm. Tom and I have no problem fostering the differences that live within our girls, yet no matter how hard we work at helping the girls establish their own sets of standards, it seems our aspie gets stung. She tries with all her might to support her sisters and enjoy their typical kinds of successes. She has become well accustomed to hanging her participant ribbons next to her sisters' first place trophies. She is accustomed to watching her sisters fly through their studies and their exams while she must work hard to maintain her marks. She is accustomed to sitting in the car with her parents while her sisters take their music lessons. She is *accustomed* to many things. But there are moments… Red hot alarms sound in my mind when I hear my aspie daughter say something to this effect, 'I could read that book if I want to, but I think it sounds stupid.' Or 'I could be in advanced math too, I just do not want to.' These kinds of comments tell us all is not totally well within our aspie. I wish comparisons and 'keeping-up-withs' weren't so important to her. But they are. And it seems there is very little we can do, at least at this point, to keep our aspie from using her sisters, especially her twin, as her mirror.

Clearly AS often steps in the path between my aspie's attempts and her successes, between her dreams and her realities; yet, I don't want her growing up blaming her AS for anything. She needs to realize her AS-related limitations are heel biting only because she is being forced to compete in an NT conscious world. I want her to know that if she were encouraged to develop her AS strengths as completely as she is encouraged to develop her NT normed strengths, she would hold the first place trophies, the highest academic grades and the biggest collection of talents ever known. And yet, as she comes to realize these truths, I worry she will turn her back on the NT world, angry and hurt in the belief that the regular world makes life too rotten for too many, too rotten for her. We become caught in a twist of thorns. It all comes back to a question of balance...

I feel my aspie daughter's angst as if it were my own, for it is common aspie territory. It was difficult for me to grow up knowing NT ways are cherished more often than aspie ways. It still is. And yet, now that I am the mother of two mostly NT children, I cannot hold firm to my old thoughts and impressions. If I did, I would inadvertently knock my NT kids around the same loop their aspie sister trips through. How odd it is for me now to respect the NT vision. How odd and how complex. I swing on the air when NT is pitted against AS, when child is pitted against child. I swing and I want to jump off before we all crash to the ground. But, of course, there is no time for the stuff tears come from. I can allow myself only a moment of collapsing despair. I have to remember crying will do me no good and then I have to turn and be off to life as it is.

I go back to my notion of balance, but this time, the parenting balance. We struggle to provide for our children according to their needs. This is a constant struggle. Life often becomes a simple question of which battles should the parents pursue? Which ones will draw the least blood? More often than not, the adults in charge know that sometimes the quickest way to closure and peace comes by avoiding the aspie's trouble spots, especially if the aspie loses control too often. For the almost NT siblings, this plan seems more like giving in than a conflict avoidance. To them it can feel as if they have been betrayed. It can seem like the aspie is the Queen in the castle, the spoiled and forceful ruler who is granted every wish, or else. *Why does Susie get everything she wants? Why does she always get to decide where we go and what we will do? Why is she always in charge?* So it must seem to the NT siblings and so it may very well be.

For our part, I know Tom and I tend to forget our aspie is not alone in her need to be told and shown she will get her way, her day and her answers. As ashamed as I am to admit this, we have to remind ourselves our NTs have those very same needs. They need their victories applauded, their efforts cheered, their struggles settled and their worries soothed. Our NTs need to hear and believe they are special, too. They need consistent reassurance that their best interests are as tied to our hearts as are their aspie sib's. In effect, we have come to see our NT girls must also be put on center stage, or else they might very well come to believe their place is behind the curtain, way back where guilt and shame lie in the wings. Our dream is for each of our girls to share the spotlight, albeit for different performances.

Of all the things we try to keep balanced for our children, I think discipline questions throw us off center more than anything else. It must seem to our mostly NTs that we let our aspie off the hook far too many times. What they are unable to see, from this side of their youth, is the real issues at the center of a problem. Tom and I try to turn every mishap into a learning experience. So, if some problem comes up because of a malicious act or conscientious decision to do harm or cause trouble, we would be set to pounce like cats on a mouse. However, if something goes wrong because of a misunderstanding or an innocent miscalculation, we would tend to turn the entire event into a learning process rather than a black and white, crime and punishment court room. While Tom and I offer probation, my NTs would say, 'You do the crime, you pay the fine.' The thing is, if we made our aspie pay the fine for every crime she committed, the poor child would be broke.

Consider the following scenario… NT sib and aspie sib are both told they can go play anywhere in the neighborhood, so long as they can see their house from wherever they are. Both kids set out for a friend's house down the block. Mom comes looking for the kids and discovers they are nowhere within sight of their home. Lo and behold she finds them at the friend's house which sits too many streets away. It is discipline time. The mostly NT sib admits that no, she could not see the house. Yes, she had wandered too far away from home. Boom. She gets grounded for a week. Fair enough. Mom turns to the aspie child.

'Didn't I tell you that you had to be able to see our house from wherever you were playing?'

'Yes,' the typically truthful aspie answers.

'Why then did you go so far away?'

'What do you mean?'

'Why did you disobey me?'

'I didn't.'

'Do not get smart with me. You clearly disobeyed me.'

'No, I didn't.'

'You know you did. You went beyond the point where you could see our house.'

'No, I didn't.'

'Quit arguing with me. Your sister admitted she could not see the house from where you were, now why are you trying to tell me you could.'

'Because I could.'

'How is that possible?'

'Easy. I climbed the roof of my friend's house and then I could see our house really good.'

Ahh…the plot gets messy. Clearly the aspie lived by the letter of the law. Was she intentionally outfoxing her mother? Probably not. Was she trying to be a smarty pants who thought herself above her mother's policy? I doubt it. Was she just being an aspie doing what comes natural to her; in other words, was she just thinking in literal terms? That would be my guess. In fact, that has been my experience. I was the child who did in fact climb the roof of a friend's house so that I could avoid breaking my mother's rule and still play where I wanted to play. I meant no harm, no insolence, no disrespect, no game. I thought I was well within the written law. Indeed, I was. What I had missed was the intent of the law. I had missed my mother's real point which was to say, I want you to stay very near the house. My punishment? I was simply told climbing on the roof is

dangerous and something I could never do again. I was also rein-
troduced to the concept of playing close to the house. My
mother explained what she had meant and from then on out, I
knew where I could and where I could not play. In this case, a
reasonable punishment, albeit barely a punishment at all, a
probation, if you will. Though I had no sibling in my story, I can
safely assume that if I had, she would have insisted she got the
raw end of the deal.

It all comes back to the beginning in the end. Sooner or later
each of our daughters will believe she has been the one who was
mistreated. This part of our equation is a mirror of every family's
equation. It is the story of siblings. As people sharing parents,
children become either three musketeers or three wet hens.
Which role the kids take on most often depends on their unique
family situation. In our case, AS plays a major role in deciding
just which role our kids will get into. It stands strong as the cord
that pulls my children together or apart. Everyday tussles like
jealousy, competition, territory struggles, and personality
conflicts take on heightened qualities that get up in the
whirlwind of our AS until they are spun perilously close to the
out-of-control mode. Incredibly intense moments pass through
our days and into our nights more often than we would certainly
like, but salvation often comes in the form of the girls' concern
for one another. When they are together, they are unquestion-
ably astounding in their support of one another. But when they
fray – the ground shakes.

KEEPING THE GROUND FROM SHAKING

○ Understand that the aspie and the aspie's siblings will
  each have their own distinct and heavy lot to bear.
  Never underestimate the load the NT child carries. NT
  children need to have an outlet for their anger and their
  confusion. The outlet could take the form of journaling,
  anger management classes, time alone with a special

friend or family member, or a 'sibling of special needs children' support group.

○ Strengthen self-esteem by: issuing well deserved compliments; putting each child in situations that will provide them a feeling of success and accomplishment; giving each child leadership roles they can handle; directly discussing the good qualities they each possess; displaying everyone's best school and art projects; attending their functions; offering kind criticism not belittling attacks; helping everyone to realize no one is perfect and that failures can be excellent ways to build character and learn something new; keeping calm in the face of over-load storms; and getting close friends, teachers and relatives also to offer their emotional and verbal support during the hard and the happy times.

○ Identify safety zones in the home where the children can go if they feel their emotional or physical safety is in jeopardy. Aspie children can be very strong and very strong willed, but so can their siblings. Reality demands each group be prepared to keep themselves isolated until a responsible adult can intervene and get things back toward the calm.

○ Be aware and on the look-out for signs of stress, anxiety and depression within the aspie and the siblings. Talk to the family's physician and school personnel to elicit their help in looking for such signs as well. Should you ever suspect anyone is tending too near any of these problems, seek counseling immediately. Never assume talk of suicide is a joke or mere threat. The suicide rate among those with AS is astoundingly high.

○ Know that any external behavior problems any of the children might exhibit could well be related to the complications inherent in a special needs family. Anger management courses, counseling, and support groups should be engaged if any behaviors begin to get anywhere near out of control.

o Realize your NT children will at some point or another come to the conclusion that you spend more time with your aspie than you do with them. Know there are valid reasons for those thoughts, even if you yourself cannot see them, but also understand that in many cases there is very little you can do to balance the scales. Perhaps honesty is once again the best policy. In the terms you need, honestly tell your NT children it is true that more of your time and attention will be spent on trying to understand, cope with and help your aspie. Compare the times you spend engaged with AS-related situations to their time with a difficult subject in school. On the other hand, do not give the NT child reason to become difficult, simply so they can then get your attention. To avoid that situation, make clear and conscious decisions to spend time with your NT child. Do not trust your memory or your best intentions to guide you to that child. Make yourself notes reminding you to ask the NT about their homework, their friendships, their days, their worries and their joys. Make a date with your NT child, record it in your schedule book and treat it as if it were a meeting you simply cannot afford to miss. Give quality when you cannot provide quantity and be sure the NT kids see the difference.

o Be prepared to cheat during those moments when the aspie completely takes over your attention. I cheat by indulging. When my aspie totally overwhelms my attention, I run to a secret toy box I keep filled with special little goodies and treats that I know my NT children will be excited about. Everything from books to special candies to puzzles to videos are in that toy box. Yes, I worry this is spoiling my children and yes I worry this is sending the message that material things can buy peace and affection, but there are times when I am desperate enough to sell my values for one smile from my NT children. If giving them a little toy keeps them occupied while I deal with a child on overload, then I will indeed give them that toy. Later, when things have calmed down, we can talk about other ways to take our minds off trauma and unhappy times. Later, when things aren't nearly as fraught with tension, we can explore some of those other ways.

o Never underestimate the power of the ripples that will run beneath your marriage or partnerships. If you do not tend to your own personal life, it will be swept up and sent away with the tide. Seek refuge and respite when you can, even if this means you both escape to the family car parked in the driveway for a few minutes now and then. Shut down your external demands when the kids go to sleep and spend that time working on your relationship. Sit in quiet together, read to one another, spend time with a mutual hobby, pass notes back and forth (the sillier the better), share a decadent dessert or beverage, and avoid any topic or behavior that might even remotely remind you of anything which causes you stress or pain. If you find you cannot manage your ripples on your own, get to someone who can help, as soon as you can. The divorce rate among special needs families couples is frighteningly high. Keep this thought close enough to prod you toward active marriage repair, but far enough away to keep it from becoming a self-fulfilling prophecy.

○ Make it crystal clear that everyone's schedules and routines must accommodate everyone else's. Work very hard to mesh the times and dates so that few interruptions and inconveniences are placed on anyone. Do not randomly sign your kids up for an after school activity. First check for conflicts that might interfere with your work schedule, the aspie's worst day of the week (usually Mondays), rougher than usual times of the year (allergy and grey, wet seasons) and any other variable you can imagine that could have a substantially rough impact on your day-to-days.

○ Whenever possible, redefine potential weaknesses as strengths. For instance, if your athletic adult aspie has a tendency to be too critical of her teammates' playing ability, see if you can convince her to be a referee of the sport instead of a player. In that role, honesty and critical thinking are well regarded and respected. If your aspie kicks and punches when she is uptight, put her in a self-defence class where those skills are married to positive attributes. Or if your young aspie is obsessed with order, assign him the household chores that require organizing, but be prepared to keep his methodology intact so that things stay put where he put them. In other words, find a creative but logical way to turn a shortcoming into a strength.

As desperate as I am to have this family be made of equal, yet independent parts, I fully understand the odds of every one of us getting an equivalent mark of control or choice, in any one situation, are minute. No, we need time and lots of it, to even out our scales. We also need compromise.

Tom and I hang on to the notion of 'compromise' like a cactus hangs on to a drizzle in the desert. We are desperate for compromise. We are at times frantic for it. But no matter how frantic we become, it is rare to see this family meet in the middle. We are

too often stuck in rigid thinking patterns and too fixed in inflex-
ibility. We are all, in those respects, very aspie-like.

Changes in routine and alterations to schedules are bound to
rock the calm of an aspie household. When it comes to establish-
ing and following routines, we know from experience that it is
imperative we allow our routines to take precedence over most
everything else, whenever possible. For instance, if one of the
girls insists we have to read a book before bed because 'we
always read a book before bedtime', we will likely comply and
read a book even if the hour is late and we are all tired. Chances
are very good the time it takes to read the book will be far
shorter than the time it would take to calm down a rigid thinker
who feels their routine has been stomped on. If we tell the kids
we will stop by the library after going to the grocery store, we
had better see to it that we do, or we had better plan on a long
night of, 'But you said we would...' arguments and attacks
because we failed to remember the plans we make are inevitably
carved in stone.

But what happens when we cannot, for any number of viable
reasons, keep our routines or our promises? How do we keep
mass chaos from breaking loose when the regular world fails to
yield to our needs? After all, we cannot really promise to control
everything that happens in life. We have to maintain some sort of
active presence in this very unpredictable world. We have to
attend school and work, we have friends we like to visit, places
we like to see and outside things we like to do, even if doing
those things causes us a tremor now and then. I suppose we
could reduce our time out in the shaky world if we were
prepared to work at home, order out for all our needs,
homeschool the girls and communicate via the internet, but we
refuse to become too reclusive too often, no matter how
tempting it may be. Tom and I both deeply believe the more our
kids, especially our aspie, practise with the regular world, the
more able they will be to deal with it on their terms. We know
that the more exposure they have to life, no matter how chaotic

it is, the less foreign and frightening it will become. We only have to look at me and the path my life has taken, to know we are correct in our beliefs.

The primary force behind our children's wanderings in the world is preparation. We never let the girls, or ourselves for that matter, start a journey of any significance without first becoming as prepared as possible for what we might see and how we might handle what we experience. We soothe our nerves with favorite stims. We work to build insightful images that fill our loose ends with the knowledge we think we might need in order to enjoy what we do. We try know as much as we can about where we will go and what we might discover. And if all else fails, we plan an escape route. In short form, we S.I.K.E. up.

THE S.I.K.E. UP

○ *Soothe.* We find everyone is more sedate in the face of challenging change if we all have a few favorite cozies with us at all times. The girls tend to keep by their sides squeeze balls, stuffed animals and a backpack filled with their favorite hand-held computer games. I travel with my purse crammed with all my usual safeties. My husband routinely goes nowhere without an armload of newspapers, a cup of something or other to drink, and his briefcase which is filled with every important paper he owns. And when we need her, we hang tight with our poodle. In fact, we have sneaked the poodle into restaurants, stores, and hotels on more than one occasion. Our motto – whatever we need to feel safe – is welcome on our trips to wherever we may go.

○ *Imagery.* When we help the aspie in us to picture, feel and hear any new avenue we plan to take, we find our collective nerves are at least soothed, if not set solidly stoic. For instance, before we go to a new friend's house, or take a vacation, or begin a new school term, we at least talk about where we are going, how we will get there, what we will most likely do once we arrive, what we are likely to eat, and what the area will look like according to the books and magazines we find on the area or the descriptions friends give us. Simply put, we never go anywhere new without first trying to picture it in our minds.

○ *The Known.* Whenever we can, we do follow the same routes to school, eat at the same time each day, follow the same living routines, stay in the same hotel chain, follow the same travel route, eat at the same restaurant chain, and visit the same kinds of stores we visit when we are at home. When that is impossible, we try to draw comparisons between the new and the old, but when we do that, we let the kids know comparisons are not perfect replicas. In other words, we prepare them to know there will be differences between the new and the old places and routines. We explain to them that we can never exactly duplicate their sets of experiences or visits.

○ *Escape.* It is very important to have a plan of rescue, should nerves get too out of control at any time, at any place. We plan and talk about what everyone can and should do if they feel their stress is mounting. Eventually, the plan becomes rote. For example, I do not even think about what I need to do when I get out of control. I instantly rock if I am sitting, sway if I am standing, 'wash' my hands in the air, talk with my fingers typing the words I am saying and rub my neck. The girls are reluctant to bring their stim needs out in public. Rather than forcing them to do so, we whisper in their ear, 'Let's go somewhere private where you can

calm down.' And then, once there, they might walk in
circles, talk a million miles a minute, jump up and
down, make vocal tics or just sit quietly and rest.

Balance that comes from mutual respect, a sense of fairness for
all, strong support, and compromise. That is our ultimate goal.
When we find it, we find a renewed sense of strength. This
strength seems especially important, for we peace-keeping,
self-esteem-building, care-giving adults need strength, strength
to spare. When I find I am tapped out and drying up, I turn to the
advice my physician gave me. 'Perhaps now is the time to
analyze your own lifestyle. Find the time to exercise. Eat decent
foods. Take a time out, every single day, no matter what. Read a
good book. Find a hobby. If you don't take care of you, who will
take care of your children?' New advice? No. Good advice? As
good as any I know.

8

Circling

It begins.
I side step through the moment
I am floating with the tiny dust dots safely quiet
until the light catches me in our dance.
Twisting with the pain, my feet unwind and slip into the stream.
The tide licks at my ankles, circling in cadence, spellbinding my
mettle
Until I am not so sure anymore.
One step too far, one step too near
I will be unfastened but will I be free?

I have a friend who likes to talk about bathroom fixtures. To him, they are the icing on the cake. I know another person who is fascinated by weather patterns; hurricane patterns, in particular. I know someone else who memorized every conceivable baseball statistic in the history of the sport. My friend's little boy is a walking encyclopedia on Egyptian history. Another friend's daughter plays her guitar through blisters and the middle of the night. My father knows more about trains and train line schedules than anyone I know. I used to know more about the Wild West than all of my peers put together. These days, I seem to know more than the average human knows about dogs and their behaviors and breed standards. My daughter collects monkeys and Winnie-the-Pooh toys. We are obsessers. For each of us, the desire to spend time and thought with a favored passion is extremely gratifying. Our obsessions are our enchanters. In the throes of our fixations we become a charmed player wrapped up with zeal and tied firm by an intensely aware ribbon of concentration. We float with our obsessions, at once nervous over the fear we might miss something essential somewhere else if we play with them too long, and then again relieved by the comfort they bring us from knowing them so well. I think of us as little ones afraid our sleep will keep secrets from us, yet oh so tired and in need of a good rest. Aspies do not always gleefully want to jump into their obsessions, but when they are there it can be the closest thing to nirvana we will ever know.

At the base, I have to wonder, are we so very different from marathon athletes, corporate presidents, bird watchers or new parents counting every breath their newborn takes? It seems lots of people, NT or otherwise, have an obsession of sorts. In my mind, that reality rests as a good one, for obsessions, in and of themselves, are not bad habits. There is much good about them. Obsessions take focus and tenacious study. They are the stuff greatness needs. I have to believe the best of the remarkable – the artists, musicians, philosophers, scientists, writers, researchers and athletes – had to obsess on their chosen fields or they would never have become great. In some respect, then, it must be said that obsessions do not have to be considered handicaps.

When I watch my child and other people engage with their obsessions, I notice more than the odd things at their hub. I notice the concentration and persistence they bring to their obsessions. I watch for the joy and contentment that will smooth their worry lines and relax their body posture and I am filled with envy, for I know they have found their moment. They have found that deep-rooted sense of fulfillment and inspiration that can only come when our interests and our fascinations and our attention mesh. It's like whirling into a vivid daydream where anything is possible and everything goes your way, a daydream you have made real. It's living in a place where we are still welcome in our own mind, a place where prejudice and pre-conceived notions of right and wrong are not at all welcome. When we give in to our obsessions, we have not given in to the NT mandate that would tell us to think in NT terms and 'act normal.'

One of the purest ways our obsessions can bring us joy comes when we use the obsession as a means toward interacting with society. How ironic, but fantastic, it is to stop and consider that which often sets the aspie apart (the obsessive interest pattern) can be the very thing that brings us close to others. Careers can be launched, advanced schooling pursued and friendships made when we use our obsessive interests as the catalyst to help us reach our goals.

ACCENTUATING THE POSITIVE SIDE OF OBSESSIONS

- Children and adults alike can often make good friendships through the people they meet at special interest clubs. I made wonderful friends during my Girl Scout years. My father enjoys lunch and field trips a few times a month with like-minded retired engineers. A friend of mine counts her birds and her bird club friends as her only friends. I believe in the importance of interest-based friendships so much, I would suggest that if there are no clubs supporting the aspie's special interest in their area, someone should start one.

- Aspies who enjoy children can look into the possibility of going to the schools to discuss their favorite obsession or share their prized collection. While the aspie might not meet a new friend during such a retreat, they can at least enjoy some time with others who are interested in hearing what they have to say and teach.

Sometimes, such a casual social relationship can be quite enough mingling for the aspie, just enough to make them feel a part of a community without getting too caught up and overwhelmed in it.

o In some cases, the obsession can be parlayed into employment. Children who grow up with a fascination for plant life might make excellent botanists. Adults totally immersed in the history of trains can make wonderful train museum volunteers or employees. People like me who are engrossed in the dog world can use their knowledge to train service or agility dogs, to breed top dogs or to become a veterinarian. Folks who adore plumbing fixtures can look into finding work in a store that sells those very items they fixate on.

o Obsessions can act as an interesting icebreaker when we meet new people, provided they are the kind that are globally enjoyed and not considered too off-the-wall. An interest in the pattern of the toilet bowl water, for instance, might not be the obsession to share with strangers; but an interest in leaf collecting might be interesting to a variety of people.

o The joy that springs from time with an obsession is to the aspie what it is to the golfer who plays eighteen holes a week. Judgment should not be leveled as to what are acceptable and unacceptable obsessions. True, there will be obsessions which might not be the best to share with a large audience, but it should still be realized that a harmless obsession should be considered just that, harmless. When push comes to shove, it should not matter too very much if an obsession appears aberrant to many in the NT world. After all, at their core, obsessions are a matter of personal interest.

If everyone were kept from their unique interests, we would all be rather dull individuals.

Despite everything I've said in defence of obsessions, reality forces me to acknowledge that my aspie needs to learn when her obsessions can surface and when they need to recede. For now, we tread gently toward that good judgment. We know there are moments when her obsessions need to take priority, and yes, times when it would be cruel and harmful to make them wait their turn. Sometimes, we even let them cut in line in front of the rest. The truth is my daughter still depends on her obsessions as I depend on a solid eight hours of sleep. She turns to her obsessions when her nerves wreck, when she is lost in space and when she is afraid of what might lie around the next bend. And should she, for some reason, forget to rely on her obsessions in situations where they could help calm her, we find them for her. For now, her obsessions mean too much to her to worry about setting concrete priority rules. Slowly, patiently, with tiny steps, we are trying to help her find the good and the bad parts of obsessing. 'It is good to play with your monkey collection when you feel badly about something that happened at school,' we tell her. 'Of course you can buy that book about monkeys because you worked hard to control your temper this whole week,' we will say. 'No, you cannot sort your monkeys right now, not until your homework is finished,' we remind her. In time, she will do these things for herself. In time she will know on her own how to share her life with her obsessions. But for now she has us to help her out.

The crust of an obsession only begins to peel into ugly sores when the person with the obsession loses control of it. When this happens, life beyond the special interest goes mute to the point where other areas of life are easily neglected or forgotten. With the obsession in charge, we begin to crave it like an addict craves a drug. Our calm behaviors are put at risk and the possibility we might lose control of anger and frustration becomes very real. When the end turns to those behaviors, life will most certainly tilt.

When obsessions make us tilt, we aspies need to learn how to ration our time; we have to learn how to prioritize properly. This is a skill for us, one that takes a great deal of time and conscious effort. Through the years, I have largely learned how to pace my time with my obsessive interests a bit more conservatively. And after much practice, much self-discipline and, most dramatically, after I had a family of my own, I finally succeeded in setting, and then following, a priority list made up of important things first. I had to learn life was about more than just me and my interests. It would be grand if I could say it was easy to put obsessions on hold for the sake of others and other things. Of course, it was not. It continues to be a very difficult task. Ants race through my blood when I have to choose between something that compels my gut and my mind, and something that holds my heart and my soul. But when I have the good sense to lean toward my heart and soul, the pay off is great. Translated into family terms, heart and soul needs mean I do not spend time with my obsessions if my family, my career or my other responsibilities need me. If I let my obsessions overtake my every move, if I let them take me away from my heart and soul, then they keep me as a prisoner. But if I use them as an oasis to turn to at the end of a busy day, or if I hold them out as a reward for having accomplished something daunting, then I keep them as I would a treasure; something to cherish and respect. The situation for me has become straightforward. Simply put, I ask myself, do I want to serve my obsessions or do I want the obsessions to serve me? The moment I realize I am not the one being served, I make my way toward ending the impact the specialized interest has on my mind and my manner.

ON NOT OBSESSING

○ Help the aspie set a reasonable time frame for spending time with obsessions.

○ Allow the aspie a reasonable time frame for talking about the obsessions with others. Along those lines, try to take an interest in the aspie's obsession while simultaneously teaching the aspie how to know when his audience is finished discussing it. Point out that engaged and interested listeners will nod, smile, ask questions, make solid eye contact and possibly even ask to touch or manipulate the obsession if that is possible. Illustrate examples of body language that suggest someone is no longer interested.

○ Make a list of rules that explain when the obsession can be visited; for instance, after homework is finished, after dinner is finished or one hour before bedtime.

○ Make a budget that will keep obsessions from getting too costly. Keep a separate envelope for the obsession savings fund. Only the money put into that envelope can be used for the obsession.

○ When it is decided the obsession is taking up too much time, costing too much money, or keeping the aspie from socializing or working on responsibilities, slowly (very slowly) begin to wean the aspie somewhat away from his interest. Reduce the time spent with the obsession by just a few minutes per day for several days and weeks, possibly even months, until the obsession is more of a memory than a habit. Simultaneously, help the aspie to replace the obsession with a new interest that might serve him better in terms of finances, socializing and prioritizing. For instance, maybe an obsession for toilet bowls could be replaced with an obsession for antique hardware. The hardware makes for more globally interesting conversation, it is easier to purchase and carry about and it is something the aspie can keep on her person, hidden from view, should she feel the need to be with the obsession while tending to other responsibilities and needs. Under no circumstances should the obsession be taken away cold turkey, unless it is proving to be dangerous in any way. No matter the reasons, I strongly believe it is a good idea to elicit the advice of a trusted counselor during any time an obsession is being curtailed or changed by someone other than the aspie.

○ Realize it is cruel and unnecessary to expect aspies to end or change their obsessions on the dot. We need to take leave of our favorite world slowly and easily. And should it ever be determined the obsession is harmful and has to be stopped as soon as possible, the advice and guidance of a qualified therapist should be sought.

Obsessions are not always reserved for thoughts and things. Many aspies are also obsessive about following specific routines. This desire should not be confused with an Obsessive Compulsive Disorder (OCD), though OCD often comes to the aspie as a secondary disorder. One way to tell the difference is to look at the reason behind the routine. Stress and anxiety are often the cause of OCD, whereas routines are often turned to because they are familiar and safe stomping grounds that have become a part of the aspie's daily pattern. Routines don't relieve us of something (anxiety) so much as they bring us to something (pleasure).

Another way to examine the difference is to explore how the person affected feels about having rigid routines. People who suffer from OCD often wish they could end their ritualistic behaviors. Aspies with favored routines are happy and in fact, often insistent that they be kept as is. Therein can lie a new problem.

A strict adherence to one or more routines can result in mass chaos. There is nothing remotely easy about trying to convince an aspie his routine can be altered, mended or ended. No sir. Routines are often the very glue that holds us together. We understand routines. They are not fickle like the NT world is. They are not multi-layered with multi-meanings like NT speech is. They bring forth the same consequences and the same emotions every time we engage in them, unlike that which happens most every time we try to engage in NT events and situations. To know how the aspie feels about our routines, think about the gentle ease with which you slip into a tradition, how often you look toward the tradition with joy and anticipation. Memories stir your belly and warm your heart when you realize you will soon be experiencing the same and the old; the familiar. Think how upset you get when the tradition is tumped on its head and changed. Maybe you're upset because Aunt Mabel decided to bring chocolate pie instead of her famous pumpkin pie to the traditional Christmas dinner, the very pie your mouth waters for all year long. Or maybe you're disillusioned because Cousin John neglected to bring his faithful guitar to the family's annual sing along. Could be you're upset because your favorite sports team changed leagues, thus ruining your end of the season cook-out with the guys from work. Perhaps you were forced to meet sadness because your children quit giving you their familiar kiss good-night. These kinds of changes appear as little things to the casual observer, but as very big things to those who have come to look forward to them.

No one likes changes in their routines, if the routines are important to them, if they bring them comfort and good feelings. So it goes for aspies who are asked to change their routines, even if the routine seems slight and unaffecting – by NT standards, that is. Aspies need to be given the sole right to decide how viable our routines are, unless of course, the routine is harmful. After all, we truly are the only persons who really know what the routine does for us. What appears as silly to an NT might very well be of extreme importance to us. When I was little, I used to refuse to step in the middle of the cement squares that led me to my school. I had to step on the cracks or step off the squares completely, no matter how muddy or wet the ground to its side was. It made me a nervous wreck to do anything else. Like many aspies, I also had a routine and rhythm attached to my eating habits. I liked to eat only one thing at a time, I never allowed two foods to touch, and I liked to eat from the twelve o'clock position all the way around in a clock-wise pattern. To this day, I still prefer my food not to touch and I often re-arrange my plate so that the first food I want to eat sits at the twelve o'clock mark.

At this point in my life, my only routine comes at bed time. Each night I follow this routine in exactly this order: I take my make-up off, floss my teeth, brush my teeth, wash the mouth guard that protects my teeth from my intense night time teeth grinding, take my medications, put on a strap of special tape that opens up my nasal passageways, put night cream on my face and hands, grab my ear plug off my night stand, fluff up two pillows for my right side and one pillow for my left side and one pillow for my head, slide onto my right side into the little alley left by my pillows, pull up the sheet first then the comforter, tuck the comforter over my shoulders but under my chin, pull up my knees around my lower right side pillow, reach behind me to nudge the left side pillow snugly behind my back, put in my ear plug and my mouth guard and TA DA, I can then look for sleep. If for some reason I am forced to alter this routine, say I lost my ear plug or was sleeping in a hotel that was too hot for a heavy comforter, I would be inside-itchy by the time I laid in my little alley. I would squirm and fidget and sigh and never find my way to a soft night. I would miss my routine and the sleep that would hide from me all night.

My father brings to my mind the best example of how comfortable routines become to those who hold them near. He has eaten for thirty-five years at the same restaurant where he orders the same exact meal day after day. The waiters greet him with his coffee and his salad prepared just the way he likes it each evening as close to 4:30 as they can be. The waiters of Dad's favorite restaurant respect his routine and even they have come to depend on it. In fact, they call should he miss a few days to be certain he is out-of-town visiting us and not at home ill. Seems to me, the waiters know how to treat a fellow who enjoys a well-worn routine. What a good lesson to copy.

When any one of my children begins a new routine, my husband and I encourage it. We believe the adherence to a routine encourages an adherence to a schedule which can be useful in terms of helping someone remember to practise a skill or complete a task or attend to a daily responsibility. We know that a house and a life filled with chaos is difficult on all of us, really. My attention deficit problems alone make it tricky for me to give in to a loosely ordered home. I'd never get anything done if I didn't have some sort of daily routine to center myself around. Each of my daughters enjoys knowing what will come next, what they have to prepare for, and what signals the end of their day. And my husband only feels safe and confident when he has woken up to his morning routine which begins with a cup of coffee and ends after two hours on his computer. Anything from that norm makes him squirm all day, so much so that he will wake himself up as early as he has to, to be sure he will have the time to complete at least those two traditions.

I feel like our life is one big circle. We try to follow the same routines as best and as often as we can. We grow attached to this special interest or that intriguing thought. In essence, we enjoy walking the same walk over and over again. Too bad for us that life keeps putting up detours.

Bumps that trip can make it even more difficult to parent successfully. I am frankly amazed by thriving single parents. I do not know how they do it. Seriously. Even with my own AS aside, I feel quite certain my effectiveness as an aspie's parent depends a great deal on the team work my husband and I are part of. We like to call our style 'Tag Team Parenting.' Though it does not always work, this plan provides Tom and me time to relax, time to rebuild our patience levels and time to ourselves. In a nutshell, Tom and I take turns being the forerunner of the childtrap. Our first step: we quickly but as accurately as we can, assess the situation at hand. In point of fact, we begin by asking the obvious questions – who is the main culprit in the problem, what is the issue at stake, how heated has the argument become and is the situation likely to dissipate on its own. From there we transition to step two: which parent leads off. Typically it is me. I am normally the quickest to rise to a conflict, the quickest to see the tiny details behind the fall. I cover my anxieties with a quiet voice that is intended to make the kids think I am filled with good patience and calm. Though they are catching on to the fact that my quiet voice is really just a technique I use to keep myself from freaking out, they still appreciate it better than the alternative. I try, as the first parent in the game, to encourage peace and compromise among the girls. It is my job to derail the out-of-control motions before they become undefeatable. I do not always make my point strong enough. If the girls are in a full blown war, a situation that many aspie families come to know far too well, I typically have no recourse but to call in Tom.

Dad's presence means things have gotten out-of-hand. When he shows up on the scene, everyone knows consequences will be met. Very specific and firmly adhered to punishments must be issued at this point. Words like, 'Or else' or 'Because I said so' go nowhere in this literal minded family. Nothing but arguments along the lines of, 'Or else what?' or '"Because I said so" is not an answer' would ensue. And while the temptation is to assume these kinds of retorts are the stuff wise-mouth behavior emanates from, we know the reality is simply that our kids have enough aspie in them to need very concrete words put before them. Their reaction to any of our subtleties is a genuine inability on their part to understand what we are trying to say. Especially in the heat of an argument or physical battle, the kids have to hear things they can instantly interpret. Vague references to rather absurdly laid out consequences go nowhere with the rigid thinkers in this family. Simply put, we cannot say things we do not mean to follow through with. Threats such as, 'If you hit your sister one more time you'll have to go to a boarding school for bad little girls,' are not interpreted as, 'We are really angry with you for hitting your sister and we will do something about it.' Rather, were our girls, the aspie in particular, to hear such a threat, they would be frozen with the thought that their parents are mean and cruel people who would willingly send them off to a kid's prison without so much as a hug goodbye. That is a train of thought that is too terrifying and too cruel for us too suggest. Threats then, cannot sneak out of our mouths.

If we are to have any control over our kids when they are out-of-control, we must lay down the law quickly and clearly. Typically, this means we remove a privilege. Spanking never did work, even when the girls were very little. More often than her sisters, our aspie would meet our attempts to spank her by spanking us in return. No, we did not appreciate that and no, we did not deal with it well at all. But that was before we had the AS diagnosis. Once we came to understand our aspie's neurological system, we knew our daughter's determination to fight us literally head on was not so much her attempt to show us she was boss as a manifestation of the fact that out-of-control behaviors are, literally, out-of-control behaviors. They are expressions of a neuro system that has sprung a leak, if you will.

We now know our aspie could no more have stopped her aggressive acts against us than she could have swum the English Channel. Even so, this knowledge did not encourage us to sit for her like a punching bag. It did, however, help us remain patient and calm when she was anything but. When it was clear spanking was not at all a wise idea for our aspie, we put a fast stop to her outbursts by doing the only thing we knew how to do – we held her firmly and tightly in an embrace until she ran out of energy. Sometimes, Tom would even lay on her with much of his body weight. Whether or not this was the right thing to do, we'll never know. But, in our case, it was the only thing we could do. No amount of time or verbal energy could stop that child from expressing herself in such a physical manner. Neither did it help to put her in a 'safe room' by herself. We never found it practical to devote one room of our home to padded walls and an empty space. No room, in our house, was completely safe. We knew if we locked her in anywhere, she would continue to lose control to an even greater extent than if we held her and forced her to settle down.

These days, our aspie has much better self-restraint. While she still carries a hefty temper, she has learned to walk away from the problem at hand and take herself to a quiet place where she can calm herself down. I asked her, not long ago, to help me find a way to tell others how she manages to calm herself and end her trauma. She said she didn't know what she could say that would help anyone. She went on to tell me she didn't really know what she did. She knew she went to her room or that she would hide in a closet someplace, but she didn't know exactly what she did beyond that. This indicates to me just how subconscious this kind of behavior really is. And it affirms to me my thoughts that we aspies do not preplan, or consciously set out, to fight with anyone. It is a gut reaction, and something we can only learn to tame when our system lets us. Until then, a tight physical embrace from a stronger and very calm and controlled individual, might be the most reasonable course of action in the face of the fury.

The toughest part about our aspie daughter's aggression always comes in the aftermath of the storm. Great amounts of guilt and frustration drip with her tears until she falls asleep totally exhausted and undone. Shivers shake her body in her fitful sleep. Her face scrunches up and her lips quiver and she screams out in woeful cries for hours, for the whole sleep. Days go by before things are back to 'normal' for her.

The over-load is always worse for her than it is for us, if for no other reason than the fact we get over it sooner than she will. To keep this little one from hating her very self for something she had very little control over, we turn to gentle reassurance. When she has finally settled down enough to hear what we are saying to her, we tell her we love and trust her no matter what happened. We tell her this is the only part of AS we wish we could change for her. And usually along the line, I will add these kinds of behaviors are part of my history too…the part it took thirty years to put behind me. With honesty and scenes from Mom's life, we illustrate when it might be best for her to leave an area. We help her to memorize which people rub her the wrong way and which of society's behaviors make her want to spit, so that she can then remind herself to stay clear of them all. And we try to help her focus on the fact that her outbursts are reactions to things that assault her. 'If you can't avoid the problem,' we tell her, 'try and rely on one of your favorite calming techniques so that you can at least weather the storm until you can get clear of it.'

By analyzing what kinds of things set her off, we hope she can simply learn to prepare herself for their onslaught. Our ultimate goal is to help her deal with whatever comes her way, no matter how impossible the situation seems at the time. It is our hope for her as she matures and gains self-control. It is our hope for her in the future.

The future. Tomorrow or the next day. Somewhere down the road. We try to paint visual pictures of the good that will come for all our girls so that they can re-color some of the memories they might be struggling to forget. One of my favorite ways to encourage good thoughts is to use humor. Nothing gets me through rough spots better than humor. I've heard it said humor hides the pain; well, whatever it does, it works to do even more than that. My sense of humor helped me make my place in this society. It is the key behind my ability to speak to large groups on the subject of AS and it is the key to laughing at my mistakes. I try desperately hard to foster a good sense of humor within my children. I don't do this through joke telling. Jokes are both hard for me to understand and thus hard for me to remember. Rather, I bring laughter to my kids by poking fun at the obvious, by exaggerating laughable details, and by tickling when tickling is allowed. I tend more toward physical comedy, the kind that has me act like a mom-clown. I stumble and change my voice and goof up my hair and put on a show for the girls. I also make fun of my mistakes in a way that falls short of self-criticism, but right on the notion that it is human to err. And when all is said and done, I remind the girls that nothing in this whole world will keep us from getting to where we want to be.

Happily, all of my girls enjoy a good laugh. As for my aspie, she is becoming a very funny young person. She has a strong wit, and a perfect sense of timing. Most important, she is learning to laugh at some of her errors, at least the kind that don't cut too deeply. If her coordination problems bring her in last in a race, she'll rise to the occasion and poke fun at her fall while congratulating the winner. If she senses she has made a *faux pas*, she will struggle to correct it by making a snappy retort. Each day, it seems, she has found even more of the confidence she needs to make light of some of life's challenges. It seems she is finally realizing some things are just not worth crying over. Some things. Not everything is a laughing matter. Like her mother, this child pales in the face of misunderstandings and misconceptions. There is nothing at all the least bit funny about our inability to miss the main idea, lose sight of the objectives or misunderstand someone's inferences and point of view. When we miss the obvious, we feel stupid and humiliated. Any laughter at that point would indeed be given only to hide the pain.

Downward slides into the out-of-control zone are unavoidable, at least in this family. The blend of tenacity, rigid thinking, sensory integration dysfunction, literal mindedness and egocentric interests makes it only natural that we would fight with life now and then. We have come to accept that about the only thing we can do to deal with that reality is to focus on the end rather than the beginning. 'We'll get through this' plays out as our motto. When, indeed, we do get through one crisis or another, we make the most of our lives together. Following the sage adage, the family who plays together stays together, we spend plenty of time just goofing off with one another.

I wish a corporation of aspies would surface that knew how to develop games and toys that were aspie friendly, for regular toys and games are often exactly what the aspie does not need. Regular physical games that capitalize on dexterity and balance and eye–hand coordination can spell disaster for aspies. So too can board games and card games that are based on out-smarting your opponent or flimsy rules that are meant to be stretched in order to win. We try to engage in big motor movement games and activities like bike riding, hiking, playing at the beach and tag. We also try to just relax together. We go to lots of movies, we spend time at libraries and bookstores, we make art projects together, and we cook together (even though two of the five of us can't follow directions to save our lives). In short, we do not try to keep up with the latest trends or the latest sports. We do what comes naturally to us – things that build on our strengths. When we are together, encouraging one another and enjoying one another, we are far more apt to smile. It is nice to circle back to a smile.

9

Sunny Side Up

Imagine the hope in a child's outstretched hand.
Find the good tucked safe between two friends sharing a walk.
Reach and make real conversations with someone
you think you do not know.
Toss back the layers that obscure innocence.
Answer the call of someone who hides.
Convince the wary to take a risk.
Redefine normal.
Make it so no one is too small to see
and
then
miracles
will be.

According to the most potent educational, medical and psychological policy makers in the world, Asperger Syndrome is a disability. I only accept the term 'disability' because it is the password that opens the doors to the support and intervention services we aspies need if we are to meet our potential. If it was practical, I would wish the word away, at least when it is used in a sentence with AS. The word comes with too many negative images. Picture – powerless, incompetent, weak, helpless, pathetic, useless, and incapable. Think – hopeless and doomed. I will not buy into the notion that AS is a dead-end diagnosis. I like to say aspies are not defective, but rather that we are simply different; differently able, if you will. Yes, we have learning inefficiencies, but never are we without the ability to learn, grow, cope and progress. Pushed further, I would assert we aspies are fine like we are, or at least we would be, if only society would learn to be more accepting and empathetic toward the a-typical. I know this kind of world could exist. I've seen it.

I was in a busy airport during one of my many business trips and, as is my norm, I was lost and largely unaware of my surroundings. Looking around without focusing on a thing, turning in short circles in search of some unknown that would bring me calm, I began to ramble to myself that I thought the airport a mess, traveling a horrible experience, and people too darn difficult to deal with on that day. People bumped into me. More than once my suitcase was bumped away from me. Frowns and furrowed eyebrows striped the faces I looked at. Heavy sighs and nasty comments came at me. My heart ran out of control. Without doubt, I know I appeared to be very easy prey for anyone who might like to pick my pocket or mug my person. While I stood nervously stimming and talking to myself under my breath, a lady stopped and asked me if I was lost. Upon my reply that I was, she calmly helped me to figure out where I needed to go and how I could best get there. She pointed at visual markers, she kept checking that I understood her directions and she built my confidence by telling me it was all too easy for anyone to get lost in such a busy place. It dawned on me right then and there that if everyone in society were as eager to lend a kind gesture as this woman was, I would always be in a state of learning and therefore, always in a state to improve my life skills and my cognitive processing. In effect, I would always be practising with a net.

When I attend AS conferences, I am routinely distressed by the aspie souls who have lost themselves in the NT/AS clash and clatter. These are the folks who stop by to talk to me with wet eyes and trembling hands. Their pain is so fresh it is all I can do to keep it from becoming my pain, too. Their life stories are echoes; I have heard them over and over again...

'I have a master's degree but no one will give me a chance at a job.'

'I want a family, but dating is difficult for me.'

'I wish I didn't have to work so hard to be accepted.'

'What's wrong with me that makes no one call me or invite me over for coffee? I won't bite them.'

'I try to do well in all my studies, but something in my brain locks up when I try to grasp something that is too abstract.'

'My family thinks I just don't try hard enough to be normal.'

'My parent/spouse/counselor/neighbor/date abused me.'

'Sometimes I want to die. Life hurts too much.'

I wonder. Does anyone in the NT world realize the pain that can come from walking against the grain? Each year we lose countless diagnosed and undiagnosed aspies to pills, bullets and booze. I hope I never know the exact numbers. I find enough reasons to be filled with fury and overcome with sorrow. And I realize that time spent on those feelings is time taken away from my attempts to make this world a safer place for my aspie daughter to slide into.

What I have to do, for the sake of my family's sanity, is focus on the positive side of AS. While I ardently remind myself to wear clothing that matches, to fix my hair, to talk in a modulated tone and not too much about any one thing, and while I do my best to teach my aspie daughter to do the same kinds of social dances, I spend the majority of my time trying to find ways to make sure she and I are happy with who we are and proud of what we are good at. For us, this translates into my tweaking the parts of our AS that the NT world might consider socially or academically undesirable, until said parts shine proud. I call this

the yin and the yang of AS. The point being this: to every trait
there are two sides. One not quite so great and one very first-rate.
For example, aspies may be seen as too blunt, but I prefer to see
them as honest and we all know honesty is the best policy. We
might be viewed as too rigid, but I think of us as people who
know what we want and what we like. Perhaps others paint us as
unemotional androids, but I would suggest people be careful
what they wish for. What frame of mind would you want your
brain surgeon to be in as he took his saw to your head? Focused
and clear of emotion or sobbing and frightened to make the cut?
What would you like of your pilots when faced with troubling
alarms? A pilot who can apply his logic to the trouble or one
who would succumb to thoughts of a fireball in the air? Can we
aspies be socially awkward? Yes, but so are many who are rather
acceptingly labeled as eccentrics. Indeed, many of history's most
eccentric personalities, particularly those in the arts, are among
the most widely admired individuals. The question has to be
re-asked: why is it seemingly so difficult for society at large to
respond to the aspie way of being? I suppose until that question
is logically *and* emotionally discussed, neither the aspies nor the
NTs will be able to meet in the middle. But when it is, I am fully
confident this place we all call home will be made much the
better.

   It seems to me, the only thing we really know about AS is that
it affects those it touches in unique ways. Oh sure, there are simi-
larities. We all share the hallmark traits – socialization problems,
semantic/pragmatic misunderstandings, odd fine and large
motor clumsiness, perseverations, obsessive interests, rigid
thinking, literal mindedness, egocentric perspectives. The thing
is, we do not all share the same mix. Each of us holds our own
secret blend of these traits, our own recipe for what makes us
tick. Add to this the gene pool, the home environment, one's
culture, gender issues and intelligence quotient, and
presto...magic occurs. What you see is not always what you get
when you look into the eyes of an aspie. Some of us present as

more traditional members of Asperger Syndrome. We stim in public, find it hard to make eye contact, speak in monologues about our favorite interests that entertain us if not you, step all over social nuances, misread the intentions of our predators as well as our heroes, struggle with sensory overloads, and typically remain in need of some sort of support. Others of us are not so different, at least on our surfaces. We can find socially acceptable stims to calm our nerves or bring us pleasure. We can learn to appear interested in others' debates, stories and lives. We can think about our interests without sharing them with an audience. We can bottle up the urge to freak out in a busy crowd until we find a quiet place that will accept our screams without judgment. We can pass job interviews and in-laws' queries with flying colors. We can find meaningful work, work at meaningful relationships, and play hide and go seek with society. These are the folks who really confuse the 'experts'. These are the ones who end up with frighteningly erroneous diagnoses that run the chronic mental illness gamut and can result, very unfortunately, in horribly inappropriate therapies. Given our many colors, is it any wonder the experts, the impressionables and the inexperienced among us are too often misinformed, misguided, and mistaken in how they handle us, the group that truly dances to a different drummer?

As convinced as I am that the aspie way of thinking is not in any way, shape or form a sub-par reality, a something that needs to be fixed or left to crumble into ruin, I would be remiss if I pretended we presented with no complications. Ours is an intricate world; one that, in spite of its many strengths, is often left tied to a tree with no discernible way to break free. It seems to me that if the NTs would learn how to accept aspies as a unique culture, rather than a defective culture that must be changed to suit the will of the many, we aspies could then put all our concentrated efforts into the things that are far more important to our beings – our mental happiness and our cognitive inefficiencies.

Ten Traits Aspies Struggle With

1. inflexible and rigid thinking

2. making connections and generalizations

3. complex problem solving

4. abstract thinking

5. multi-tasking

6. expressing emotions

7. reading non-verbal messages

8. making sustained and appropriate eye contact

9. change in routines or transitions

10. language and communication which goes beyond a literal level

The size of the struggle depends on many things. When I look back at my young years, I can recall knowing I did not enjoy the same kinds of activities my peers did and that I had trouble understanding abstract concepts. I often felt misunderstood and I usually left a conversation feeling somewhat confused. I suppose I recognized I was a different kind of kid, but my parents were so very good at convincing me I was fine and good and capable that I never dwelled on my struggles to the point they overwhelmed me – until I went off to college and left my family and peers behind. Only then did I realize just how different was my way of functioning and my way of understanding the world. Only then did I face some of the sadness and pain many with AS face throughout their lives.

As tough as it was for me to face each of my inefficiencies, I think that, in the long run, the experience was much more than insightful. It was therapeutic and cathartic. The knowledge that my neurosystem was responsible for so many of my differences gave me the freedom and strength to search earnestly for coping methods and friends who would help me learn and grow. Nowadays, I apply my intellect to everyday happenings, so that logic and problem-solving analysis provide me with the answers to life's questions. It doesn't really matter to me that I have to 'think' my way through my days while other people instinctively know how to act and what to do when faced with similar situations. Sure there are times when I get utterly exhausted from the constant analyzing and re-structuring and dependence on others' advice. But I figure everyone has something that exhausts him or her.

When I am particularly over-loaded by my AS struggles, I quickly think about those who are more affected than I am. In particular, I think about my daughter. If I find it hard to fix my mind on the big picture rather than the teensie tiny details that catch my fancy first and foremost, how hard must it be for my daughter to lose sight of the little things so that she can see the really important? When I am told I totally missed someone's intent, I worry: how much of what my daughter hears, does she really and truly understand? On the days my routine is slip-slopped, I cannot help but look at my aspie to see how much more rattled she is than I am. If I am really shaken up, she must surely be ready to spill. The moment my body refuses to follow what my mind tells it to do, I am reminded of how hard my aspie has to struggle to be accomplished in her favorite sport. The list goes on. The longer it gets, the more apprehensive I become. The challenge becomes one of pushing the apprehension into action. It becomes a matter of risk taking.

Risk takers are everywhere, but not so proportionately in the AS community. We tend to be stifled by approach avoidance and a strong rejection of failure. We might come close to trying something new, but then immediately avoid the event for fear we will fail and fail miserably. I presume this tendency is in many ways directly related to our self-esteem and our self-confidence level, but I also suspect it has some relationship to our intolerance for error and our reliance on predictability, as well. We do not like it when things turn up wrong and we don't appreciate it one bit when things do not go according to our plan. The combination makes for little risk taking.

Dr Tony Attwood told me during one of our many visits that he thought much of my social success comes from the fact that I often do take risks. I am not certain why risk taking comes readily to me, but I suspect it is because my parents always encouraged me to try new things and go new places. Their trust in total immersion and inclusion provided me with safe opportunities that taught me, even when I messed up, that life would go on and so will I. Perhaps most important, they allowed me to define what was risky and what was not. If I thought that going to a roller-skating rink was frightening, they acknowledged this apprehension and did not dismiss it as silly or unreasonable. They knew my definition of risk was the definition that mattered the most.

HELPING ASPIES TO TAKE A RISK

○ Educate them about the situation you hope they will try to participate in, well in advance of the time the activity will actually occur. Taking the mystery out of an unknown can do much to reduce stress and apprehension.

○ Present them with logical and honest support statements that underscore that it is ultimately up to them whether or not they decide to continue with the activity. Help them to set a reasonable set of expectations concerning the event, and promise them that if the event doesn't meet most of those expectations after a certain period of time or effort, they can stop participating in it.

○ Give the aspie a 'Time out' signal they know they can use the moment the situation gets too overwhelming. If they use the signal, be sure to honor it and get them out of the activity as soon as you can.

○ Consider ways the aspie might engage in the activity little by little at first and until she becomes comfortable with it, segment by segment. For instance, if the aspie wanted to try and play an individual sport (team sports present a whole other set of interesting dynamics and risks), she could begin by first watching the sport on television a few times. The next step could be taking a few private lessons with one instructor. When a comfort level is met at that point, she could move on to a small group lesson with children the instructor has hand picked because of their calm or kind temperaments. Then a play date with one of those children might be made so the two can enjoy the sport together. Eventually, it might be possible for the aspie to engage in competition or a regular day out for playing the sport with a few other kids.

○ Remind the aspie of situations she once dreaded because she thought them too risky, but that she now engages in on a regular basis. Compare the activities and illustrate how her feelings and perceptions eventually changed as the situation unfolded and made her feel more comfortable over time. For example, you could say: 'Lots of things are scary at first. Remember the first time you went to Girl Scouts? You really didn't want to go! We had to promise you an ice cream cone if you would go. We did that two times before you decided Girl Scouts was a fun activity. Now you really enjoy it. You met a good friend there, you think earning badges is cool, and even look forward to the field trips they take. If you had given up on Girl Scouts, look what you would have missed.'

o Ask a positive role model to share his or her experiences with a similar risk taking experience, so long as the outcome was positive. While it is reasonable and responsible to be honest about the difficulties, it is questionable if the aspie would want to go ahead with a risk, if he knew his role model failed miserably at it.

o Use one of the aspie's interests to propel him into a rather risky situation. If the aspie likes airplanes, for example, it might be possible to get him to the point where he can join a radio controlled model airplane club.

o Listen to your aspie. If he tells you either with his verbal or nonverbal messages that the activity is too hard to imagine doing, do not force the issue. One horrible experience can be more than enough to make it impossible to return to something.

o If the event turns out to be a disaster, and some inevitably will, provide lots of emotional and rational support. Give the aspie time to regroup, allow her to blow off steam, help her find ways to control her anger or fear, and if you even suspect that some deep down damage has been done, enlist the help of a professional.

I don't know why my early education and upbringing made my being so receptive to risk and change. I know dozens of wonderful parents who work very hard to help their aspies, often to no obvious avail. For any number of reasons – a below average IQ, weak peer relationships, inappropriate academic settings, and additional neurological, psychological and/or learning problems – some aspies seem to be more resistant to intervention and change than others. For these folks, I strongly suggest a team of experts in the fields of speech and language pathology, occupational therapy, cognitive psychology, neurology and special education be pulled together to develop a global plan that is capable of peeling back the layers of struggles one by one, so that each gets the remediation deserved. Never should anyone simply assume all aspies move along the spectrum to near-NT all on their own. Always should optimism be held out that aspies can learn how to take control of their own destiny. Finally, it has to be said that there are multitudes of aspies who will never want to change a thing about whom they are. It is my opinion that these aspies deserve the right to hold tight to that belief.

I often say that, if I could, I would go back to a day when my AS was more obvious. No, I would not want to be filled with the anxiety that used to bring me to overloads and I would not want to be any more affected by sensory stimuli than I still am, but I do wish I could snuggle into the world that used to be so private and serene; the kind of world that only really comes to those who know how to disappear. But, those days seem too far behind me to grasp any more. I think my level of self-awareness makes it almost impossible to return to the old me. I am too fully aware of the fact that my children and spouse depend on me to be pretty close to NT now that I am theirs.

My level of self-awareness often brings comment from those who study AS. I am told that my ability to self-analyze is a strong factor in my ability to learn NT ways. Some have told me this is typically a more female than male attribute, be the individual aspie or NT. Even so, there are many aspies, both male and female, who never quite realize their AS inefficiencies have any impact on the struggle life shows them. They wind their way through life never realizing nor coming to terms with their innate separation from NTs. They may never know why they were denied a job or kept from a party or were never able to form a lasting interpersonal relationship. Thoughts will come that whisper other reasons totally beyond the AS. Blame might be placed on a weak academic transcript or awkward timing or fate. The idea that they are unable to fit in and follow the trends and thinking patterns of NTs might float on the peripheral, but then again, it might be as far from the conscious as it could be.

I have met countless parents and spouses, teachers and counselors who tell me they cannot possibly help the aspie in their life because the aspie will not acknowledge there is anything wrong with their way of being. I cannot help but wonder if the adjective 'wrong' is part of the problem. We aspies do not view ourselves as wrong. Different, probably, at least on some level. Wrong? No. I suggest to those who are anxious about helping the aspie toward deeper self-awareness, that perhaps they could find a more positive way to enlighten the aspie about his communication skills, socialization methods and affective style. In our family, we always encourage our aspie to realize she is filled to the brim with admirable traits and powerful abilities, yet we are equally as faithful in trying to get her to be aware of her social, emotional and cognitive inefficiencies. Keeping the balance of the power such that we help her to work from her strengths, we present her with academic and affective strategies geared to help her turn her inefficiencies into firm proficiencies. Our goal is to help our daughter do what my father and I were able to do, join the world on its terms without losing sight of who we are and what we need.

HELPING A MISPLACED ASPIE SEE WHERE SHE IS COMING FROM

o Rely on logic, and not emotional explanations, when discussing the differences between the aspie's way of thinking and the NT way of thinking.

o Refrain from using words that send negative connotations when describing the way the NT world views the aspie.

○ Address one point at a time, realizing too many points at once will leave the aspie overwhelmed and under-confident.

○ Try to remain as concrete as possible. Abstract analogies and metaphors might just leave the aspie more confused than ever.

○ Spend at least as much time talking about the strengths of the aspie as you do the inefficiencies.

○ Consider using a written dialogue rather than a spoken dialogue, so the aspie will have adequate time to process the information rationally.

○ Use graphics to help you make your points. Think lists: cause and effect equations with arrows, plus/minus and equal signs; simple drawings that illustrate simple emotions such as happiness and sadness; font changes such as all caps to express confusion and italics to represent frustration and all lower case to express sadness; photos that catch the aspie in AS mode, perhaps standing too close to someone, too far removed from a group, avoiding eye contact, etc.

○ Be careful you do not push the aspie farther than she can go. Too much self-analysis, too quickly, can be terribly devastating. If you are the least bit concerned about how the aspie will react to your efforts, immediately enlist the help of a qualified third party to help you intervene.

Maybe it would help everyone involved if aspies began a big advertising campaign to tout our exceptionalities. If our supporters knew more about our fortes, wouldn't they be better prepared to help us learn how to depend upon and use our strengths for learning new things and developing new well-being strategies? When my daughter is disappointed in herself because she cannot discern what the main idea of a story is, we tell her that though this is important and something she needs to continue to work on, her ability to pick up the most minute details makes her especially strong at figuring out the answer to who dun-it in mystery novels. If she expresses sadness over friends she has lost because she told on them for doing something they should not have, we try to tell her there are two kinds of tattle-tales: one tells on others to get them in trouble, the other tells on them to keep them safe from harm or to help them learn right from wrong. So long as she fits the definition of the last descriptor, we praise her for her concern and then help her to figure out how she can keep others out of harm's way without getting them into trouble. Simply put, we try to focus on the good part of aspie.

TWENTY FIRST-RATE WAYS TO DESCRIBE ASPIES –
ASPIES ARE:

1. very loyal

2. open and honest

3. guardians of those less able

4. detail oriented

5. uninterested in social politics

6. often witty and entertaining

7. capable of developing very strong splinter skills

8. storage banks for facts and figures

9. tenacious researchers and thinkers

10. logical

11. enthusiastic about their passionate interests

12. able to create beautiful images in their mind's eye

13. finely tuned in to their sensory systems

14. ethical and principled

15. dependable

16. good at word games and word play

17. inquisitive

18. rule followers

19. unambiguous

20. average to above average in intelligence.

The 'good part of aspie'. I like that. It doesn't overshadow the fact that there are real issues aspies must learn to deal with, but at the same time, it nudges one to figure out that AS is not the end. There is no question that for me and mine, life is significantly better when sights are set on the positive points of AS. My daughter and I are often asked what we like best about being an aspie. Some days that question is harder to answer than other days. But every day, we do have an answer. My aspie daughter particularly likes the fact that she is such a good rule follower, because she knows it is very important to spend her life doing right by society, rather than wrong by it. Most days, both of us take pride in the fact that we are very loyal people who will support those we care about to the nth degree. As for me alone, I am happy for my tenacious interest in my intellectual pursuits. I am proud of the knowledge I possess and I am always anxious to learn even more. But of all the AS traits we have, I can easily say the one that strikes me as the most impressive is the one I call 'sensory assemblies'.

Sensory assemblies take the thoughts to spots only aspies can really relate to. In effect, the concept refers to our tendency to gather up the world by its collection of sensations. For instance, nuances of everyday things can come to my mind until they are far more enchanting than the chunk of the main scheme. I can get happily lost in the most minute of things, contentedly teasing out the fine points into even tinier wedges for my appreciation… A table is a table to an NT. But to me, it is a texture-rich playground for all of my senses to take pleasure in. I can run my hand across its lines, measuring it for symmetry, feeling it for bumps and crannies carved from the surface and jostling it for the kind of music that comes when I thump it or scrape it with my fingers. I can lean down and smell the wood or the wood's polish and quickly find a memory attached to that smell, maybe even a memory that sends me on a perfect visit to something wonderful I had all but forgotten. I can center my attention on a piece of the table, say a decorative cut-out or an arch of a corner, and turn that least of things into a complete element totally valuable in and of itself. A table. Perhaps nothing tremendous in the big scheme of things, but take that table and see instead a mountain range waiting to be painted or a computer program ready to take shape or a medicinal formula on the verge of discovery. Imagine how sensory assemblies can twirl and seep into the crevices and crannies of all sorts of complex problems and puzzles. Consider now, the special wisdom the aspie could bring to humanity.

With every aspie, there comes a unique understanding of how things mix and mingle. This is a character trait that needs to be fostered and appreciated. It is true, the aspie will not always jive with the rituals of society, but is that the most important thing in our collective stuffing? Is it really?? For me, it is as simple a question as this: should aspies truly be made to bend until we almost break, or should everyone with all sorts of neurological make-ups be enabled and encouraged to share their individual visions in such a way that we might all benefit from the experience?

I have great hope that when all is said and done, when all the data has been gathered and all the recommendations have been made, aspies and NTs will finally discover that they have far more to offer one another than either of them ever realized. Together, they will then know, anything is possible.

Epilogue

My family is a dot-to-dot family. As pieces, we appear disjointed and unconnected, but when we build lines between us, our single dots link and mesh and complement one another. In most ways, our AS is a mere matter of fact, a something we have always held. In the main, I suppose, we do not really do anything so very different from other families when we take things on the whole. We enjoy each others's company, we do nice things for each other, we celebrate together, we fight over who gets to sit in what chair, what television show we will watch, what we will eat for dinner, which book we will read as a family. We mix and match and squabble and make-up just like families are supposed to. Yet… we would be kidding ourselves if we thought we met life's situations with the same set of reactions neurotypical families do. We are different in the way we perceive the world. We may learn how to mimic and mirror the NT world, but we remain mystified by it.

As I turn new pages in my life's book, I make notes in the margins. I know I cannot learn everything I need to know about others or even myself without taking notes. These notes make up my working agenda. Like a living diary, they guide me and lead me. The given, is not given to me. It remains apart. Elusive. Imagine…volumes upon volumes of discourse, either tangible words bound between trustworthy leather covers, or mind's eye words bound between the heart and the soul ready and able to tell us how to talk, walk, dress, behave, respond, initiate, think. Wouldn't such a library make life easier for everyone, the NTs and the aspies and everyone in-between?

I know the words in this book do not comprise a library, but I do trust they comprise at least a translation of what it can mean to be aspie. Aspie. I have grown rather attached to that word. I like the way it sounds. I like the way it rolls off my lips as if I am whispering a grand secret, for in some ways that is exactly what I am doing, the moment I sound the word aloud. Aspie tells my secret for it describes who I am...in an elastic sort of way. It does not lock me in to a norm. It does not toss me to the bull's-eye. It does not make me this or that. Rather, it gives me freedom to experience the world in threefold measure where everything that might be one thing to most becomes a completely new entity to me. To my mind, being an aspie means being able to ferret out details that might otherwise go unknown. It means searching for reason and logic and truth behind the hidden curtain and the magic mirrors NTs play behind. It means spending real time and effort on those interests and hobbies and ideas that can wake sleepy dreams and capture all the attention from daydreams. It means loyalty to those people and those ideas we care about. It means tenacity and perseverance despite the hills and the valleys. And it means different...not less, not bad, not unworthy or incapable...just different. Yes. I like my life defined by the noun, aspie.

I regret there are those in the regular world who do not deeply understand what it means to be an aspie. For that reason, and I suspect many more, they are not always certain how to respond to us, how to talk to us, look at us, work with us, be with us. I find myself wondering if that might be the case not only because they find us complex, but also because we find them equally as fuddled. Both groups seem woefully unable to conceptualize an accurate theory of the other's mind. The challenge, as it were, becomes how two such innately different populations can find a way toward the same playing field.

I sincerely hope this book provides the answers to some of those challenges.

LHW

Appendix I
Web Resources

- Liane Holliday Willey's home page: www.aspie.com
- Tony Attwood's home page: www.tonyattwood.com
- NLD (Non Verbal Learning Disorder) on the web: www.nldontheweb.org
- Asperger Syndrome Coalition of the United States, Inc.ASC-U.S.: www.asperger.org/
- Action for Autism Spectrum Disorders: www.actionasd.org.uk/
- Online Asperger Syndrome Information & Support: www.udel.edu/bkirby/asperger/
- The Gray Center for Social Learning and Understanding: www.TheGrayCenter.org
- Prelude Music Therapy: www.home.att.net/~preludetherapy/index.html
- MAAP (More advanced individuals with Autism, Asperger's Syndrome, and Pervasive development disorder): www.saintjoe.edu/~daved/MAAP/
- Future Horizons: www.futurehorizons-autism.com
- Jessica Kingsley Publishers: www.jkp.com

Appendix II

Australian Scale for Asperger's Syndrome Second Edition[*]

The following questionnaire is designed to identify behaviours and abilities indicative of Asperger's Syndrome in children during their primary school years. This is the age at which the unusual pattern of behaviour and abilities is most conspicuous. Each question or statement has a rating scale with 0 as the ordinary level expected of a child of that age.

A. Social and Emotional Abilities

1. Does the child lack an understanding of how to play with other children? For example, unaware of the unwritten rules of social play.

2. When free to play with other children, such as at school lunchtime, does the child avoid social contact with them? For example, finds a secluded place or goes to the library.

3. Does the child appear unaware of social conventions or codes of conduct and make inappropriate actions and comments? For example, making a personal comment to someone but the child seems unaware how the comment could offend.

4. Does the child lack empathy, ie. the intuitive understanding of another person's feelings? For example, not realising an apology would help the other person feel better.

5. Does the child seem to expect other people to know their thoughts, experiences and opinions? For example, not realising you could not know about something because you were not with the child at the time.

6. Does the child need an excessive amount of reassurance, especially if things are changed or go wrong?

7. Does the child lack subtlety in their expression of emotion? For example, the child shows distress or affection out of proportion to the situation.

8. Does the child lack precision in their expression of emotion? For example, not understanding the levels of emotional expression appropriate for different people.

9. Is the child not interested in participating in competitive sports, games and activities.

10. Is the child indifferent to peer pressure? For example, does not follow the latest craze in toys or clothes.

B. Communication Skills

11. Does the child take a literal interpretation of comments? For example, is confused by phrases such as 'pull your socks up', 'looks can kill' or 'hop on the scales'.

12. Does the child have an unusual tone of voice? For example, the child seems to have a foreign accent or monotone that lacks emphasis on key words.

13. When talking to the child does he or she appear uninterested in your side of the conversation? For example, not asking about or commenting on your thoughts or opinions on the topic.

14. When in a conversation, does the child tend to use less eye contact than you would expect?

15. Is the child's speech over-precise or pedantic? For example, talks in a formal way or like a walking dictionary.

16. Does the child have problems repairing a conversation? For example, when the child is confused, he or she does not ask for clarification but simply switches to a familiar topic, or takes ages to think of a reply.

C. Cognitive Skills

17. Does the child read books primarily for information, not seeming to be interested in fictional works? For example, being an avid reader of encyclopaedias and science books but not keen on adventure stories.

18. Does the child have an exceptional long term memory for events and facts? For example, remembering the neighbour's car registration of several years ago, or clearly recalling scenes that happened many years ago.

19. Does the child lack social imaginative play? For example, other children are not included in the child's imaginary games or the child is confused by the pretend games of other children.

D. Specific Interests

20. Is the child fascinated by a particular topic and avidly collects information or statistics on that interest? For example, the child becomes a walking encyclopaedia of knowledge on vehicles, maps or league tables.

21. Does the child become unduly upset by changes in routine or expectation? For example, is distressed by going to school by a different route.

22. Does the child develop elaborate routines or rituals that must be completed? For example, lining up toys before going to bed.

E. Movement Skills

23. Does the child have poor motor coordination? For example, is not skilled at catching a ball.

24. Does the child have an odd gait when running?

F. Other Characteristics

For this section, tick whether the child has shown any of the following characteristics:

(a) Unusual fear or distress due to:

ordinary sounds, eg. electrical appliances
light touch on skin or scalp
wearing particular items of clothing
unexpected noises
seeing certain objects
noisy, crowded places, eg. supermarkets

(b) A tendency to flap or rock when excited or distressed

(c) A lack of sensitivity to low levels of pain

(d) Late in acquiring speech

(e) Unusual facial grimaces or tics

If the answer is yes to the majority of the questions in the scale, and the rating was between two and six (ie. conspicuously above the normal range), it does not automatically imply the child has Asperger's Syndrome. However, it is a possibility and a referral for a diagnostic assessment is warranted.

This copy of the ASAS was downloaded from www.tonyattwood.com, with the permission of Tony Attwood.

Appendix III

Fast Facts for Those
New to Aspie World

Aspies are:

- ○ visual thinkers
- ○ literal thinkers
- ○ routine oriented
- ○ inflexible thinkers
- ○ weak socializers
- ○ more truthful than not
- ○ rule oriented
- ○ obsessive about their favorite interests
- ○ principally unable to understand others' point of view

Aspies tend to:

- ○ have low self-esteem
- ○ enjoy time spent with older and younger people more than time spent with their same age peers
- ○ interrupt people while they are in mid-sentence
- ○ find eye contact a difficult skill to master
- ○ have very vivid nighttime dreams
- ○ have poor executive functioning skills
- ○ have average to above average IQ's

- find it difficult to do more than one task at a time
- be uncoordinated
- have a high pain tolerance
- be very ethical and moral
- find introspection very difficult
- be very vulnerable to stress
- vocalize their inner thoughts
- find emotions difficult to discuss or understand
- have difficulties with interpersonal relationships
- have strong verbal skills
- copy others' behaviors, words, accents and appearance

Aspies often have confounding problems including:

- Central Auditory Processing Disorder
- Hyperlexia
- Attention Deficit Disorder or Attention Deficit Hyperactive Disorder
- Sensory Integration Dysfunction
- Non-Verbal Learning Disorders
- Semantic Pragmatic Language Disorder
- Obsessive Compulsive Disorder
- Depression
- large and small movement disorders

Appendix IV
Self-Affirmation Pledge for Aspies

- I am not defective. I am different.
- I will not sacrifice my self-worth for peer acceptance.
- I am a good and interesting person.
- I will take pride in myself.
- I am capable of getting along with society.
- I will ask for help when I need it.
- I am a person who is worthy of others' respect and acceptance.
- I will find a career interest that is well suited to my abilities and interests.
- I will be patient with those who need time to understand me.
- I am never going to give up on myself.
- I will accept myself for who I am.

Appendix V

Self-Affirmation Pledge
for Aspie Parents

I will endeavor to...

- see the world through my aspie's eyes.
- seek professional help the instant things move beyond my ability to cope or understand.
- become my child's strongest advocate.
- find no shame in my aspie's behavior, disregarding the advice of others that does not fit.
- laugh when I can laugh.
- give in to sadness only when I must.
- establish a strong support team.
- remain optimistic about my child's future.
- look both ways when I parent, keeping in mind all my children need me.
- find time for my significant other.
- take time for myself.
- encourage my child's strengths far more often than I try to restrict them for their weaknesses.
- savor the good and ride the tide through the not so good.
- lay an end to blame and guilt.
- realize there is a world beyond Asperger's Syndrome.

Appendix VI
Making Sense of Small Talk

Aspies are renowned for our difficulties with small talk. Objectively speaking, it seems to me that aspies tend to pepper their talk with far more outwardly inappropriate verbalizations than their NT counterparts do. My own self-analysis pointed me to seven communication problem areas I believe I share with my aspie friends. They are: brusqueness, intrusiveness, egocentrism, inappropriateness, pedantry, disjointedness and insensitivity. There may be more or there may be less, but I would wager the majority of our tangled commentaries can trace their roots to one of the seven.

Aiming to find a way to make aspie talk more in-fitting with NT small talk, I thought it might be useful to illustrate examples of common small talk exchanges as they might be when presented by an aspie, and as they could be if they were devoid of whatever flaws they might have. In other words, a 'before and after' presentation. For purposes of simplicity and illustration, the imperfect exchanges will each only contain one of the seven flaws I noted above.

In order to make this appendix a useful exercise, I would suggest a trusted friend or confidant of the aspie go through the given exchanges, stopping to discuss the pros and cons of each one in whatever detail seems necessary in order to underscore good comprehension. For example, after reading the comments 'This party is boring; I'm leaving now,' someone might point out that though the comment may have been honest and to the point, it was also too blunt and insensitive. All this in the hopes that once the aspie objectively studies the presented discourse, she will be able to apply new and perhaps kinder-seeming rules to her own speech. One note – before this kind of study begins I think it is important that the aspie understand she is not personally under any kind of critical attack. I would go to great lengths to let the aspie know this is about helping her make sense to NTs in a way they can understand. My husband and I try very hard to tell our daughter it's not so much what she is trying to say to others, but rather, how she says it, that makes or breaks her small talk with friends and teachers. So when she says, 'But I didn't mean to hurt anyone's feelings', we can assure her we are sure she didn't, but that no matter her intent, words can hurt and because of that, they have to be chosen very carefully. Once we've taught her to understand what she means isn't necessarily what NTs hear, we believe she will go a long way toward finding a good common ground to talk on. One more note – most of the following 'before' examples were indeed spoken by me…before I designed this small talk scheme.

Small Talk One: Entering or leaving a conversation

I am never quite sure how to start or leave a conversation. I seem to be more inclined to forget introductions. I have to remind myself that there are certain rules society lays down regarding how we approach and leave a conversation. Like many aspies, I tend to verbalize everything that is on my mind, no matter what the topic, no matter who I am standing by, no matter if I know the person or not. I also know plenty of aspies who walk away from a conversation in mid-sentence. Too many times, I have seen them either turn and walk away before the person they are speaking to has finished what they are trying to say, or walk away themselves even though they are still carrying on the conversation. It makes me think the aspies forget conversations have beginnings, middles and ends – in that order. When I talk to others, I consistently picture a diagram of a conversation that is built around beginnings and endings I have memorized. I typically assume the middle will take care of itself if I remember all the other little rules I talk about in this appendix.

Before	After
I am so fat. I eat as much as my husband does.	Isn't it hard to shop at the grocery store without buying junk food? Even though I think I'm overweight, I buy some of the most fattening foods. And wouldn't you know I end up eating more of it than my husband.
Do you know me?	Have we met before?
I don't know you. Who are you?	Hi. My name is _. I haven't seen you here before. Are you new to the area?
I don't want to talk to you any more. Goodbye.	It's been interesting talking to you. Goodbye now.
This party is boring. I'm getting out of here.	Gee. Look at the time. I better be leaving.

Small Talk Two: Using appropriate transitions

This can be very tricky, but the main idea is to build a bridge between topics so that listeners aren't left chasing ideas wondering what will come next and what happened to the thought before. Every time I talk to people, I try to remind myself to keep my mind from jumping around too often. To keep myself on track, I also try to incorporate questions into my paragraphs so the other people I'm talking to can jump in and have their turn to talk. Otherwise, like many aspies, I find I tend to monologue and hog a conversation that has too many disjointed bits and pieces. My last trick along these lines is to try and add more background information than I would think is necessary, even at the risk of sounding too chatty. It's all about my realizing others cannot read my mind. Others need to have a bit of fill-in, in order to understand where I am coming from.

Before	After
I have a great dog at home. He's a Newfoundland. He's a giant breed. I don't know why I can't take my dog into public places. People in public can be so rude. Parking lots are the worst. I hate it when handicapped spaces are taken by people without handicaps. I don't think of myself as handicapped. Just differently abled. When I look at the sky I wonder how those birds are able to fly. Isn't that the most miraculous thing?	I have a great dog at home. He's a Newfoundland. He's a giant breed. I don't know why I can't take my dog into public places. Speaking of the public, do you find some people just plain rude? (*At this point the topic has changed. This makes it a good time to let the other person speak.*) [Assume the other speaker said they did think people in public can be rude.] It makes me so mad when I see someone who isn't handicapped parking in a handicapped space. Which reminds me, I know people who consider Asperger Syndrome to be a disability. I don't. I see myself as differently abled. Saying the words, 'differently abled' made me think of how miraculous it is that birds can fly. Don't you agree? (*Once again the topic has changed and once again this is a good time to let someone else speak.*)
Make sure when you go outside today you have your hat and gloves with you. It is freezing and you could get frost bite within seconds. I have to go to the store for some milk. Where did I put my coffee? I need to clean this house. It is getting out of hand.	Make sure when you go outside today you have your hat and gloves with you. It is freezing and you could get frost bite within seconds. I need to go out too! I need some milk. I would have liked to have put milk in my coffee, but since I'm out I couldn't. Where did I put my coffee? I am having a hard time finding anything in this house. It is getting out of hand.

Small Talk Three: Articulating general opinions

As hard as it was for me to believe, I have finally learned to realize most people, especially people I only talk small talk to, don't really want to know all of my opinions. This is one of the hardest parts of communicating for me. I find it very stifling to talk without stating my opinions. To work around that difficulty, I try to find ways to state my opinions gently and without too much force. I try not to be too blunt and I try to coat my opinions with nicety phrases like 'I believe' or 'I could be wrong, but' or 'maybe' or 'I'm not sure, but'. I also rely on what I call 'account-ability questions' more than declarative statements when I want to get my opinion out in the open. These types of questions encourage people to analyze their own behavior so that I can at least appear to be an objective bystander rather than a curt accuser. These methods are not foolproof. When I find that I have been too blunt or too opinionated, I always apologize and explain that I didn't mean to act like a rude know-it-all. In other words, I try to keep myself from appearing as a person who is too opinionated to listen to others or too egocentric to care about what others might have to say. Be that as it may, I really find it impossible to keep all my opinions to myself. I guess I see no point in talking at all, if I'm not able to say what is on my mind. Any other kind of talk seems pointless to me. Still and all, I have learned to temper my desire to speak my mind…at least a tiny bit.

Before	After
You should not be taking that big of a suitcase on the plane. You need to check that bag because it is clearly too big for the overhead compartment. Go do that now!	Gosh. That suitcase looks rather large. Are you sure it will fit in the overhead compartment? Maybe you should not try to bring it on board with you.
There is no way you are going to serve me that sandwich after handling the money. You need to wash your hands first. I cannot even imagine the germs that must be on your hands right now. Please throw that sandwich away and make me a new one.	Excuse me but I didn't see you wash your hands before you started to make my sandwich. I noticed you were handling money a minute ago. Would you please wash your hands and make me a new sandwich. I am really afraid of germs. Thanks!
I am trying to talk. Why do you keep interrupting me? Can't you see my mouth is moving? When I am done, you can tell me what you need to tell me. Until then, you need to close your mouth.	It seems like we are both trying to talk at the same time. Let's take turns. If you don't mind, I'll go first because if I don't I'm likely to forget what I wanted to say! When I'm done I'll ask you what it was you wanted to tell me. Is that OK by you?

Small Talk Four: Fitting dialogue to the situation

I know full well how much energy it takes to keep small talk on the NT acceptable track. Sometimes it takes so much effort, it leaves me overwhelmingly exhausted. Thankfully, I do have friends and family members who accept my AS talk as it comes out, totally unaltered or tempered. With those folks I can be me, odd statements, questionable affect, bluntness and all. To quote my husband who receives more of the real me than anyone, 'If I didn't like it, I wouldn't be married to you.' Alas, he doesn't echo the sentiments of everyone who hears my voice. What I now know is this: the audience is as important as the message, maybe even more so. When an aspie sets to speak, she must realize who she is talking to will make as many demands on her words as anything else possibly could. Generally speaking, I think there are three main audience categories we need to be aware of, so that we can tailor our speech to fit the cause and keep us out of trouble. Group one would include people in authority such as bosses, teachers, police, judges and doctors. Group two would encompass people one only associates with during work or day-to-day general activities including co-workers, neighbors, store clerks and virtual strangers one would meet while standing in line or walking in a park. Group three envelopes the close people, the interpersonal friends and family members.

Before	After
Are you out of your mind? I did not throw that can of trash out onto the street. I never break any law and I would certainly never pollute the environment. Now leave me alone.	**(Group One)** I don't mean to sound impertinent, but I can promise you I did not throw any trash out on the street. I would never pollute. I will be glad to pick up the trash because it is the right thing to do, and then I'd like to get back to my work if that's all right. **(Group Two)** It may look like I was the person responsible for polluting our street, but I have to tell you that I would never pollute the environment. I'm going to go ahead and pick it up though because I can't stand to think of this trash being out here. **(Group Three)** Are you out of your mind? Do you really think I could ever pollute? Surely you know how important the environment is to me? Now help me pick this mess up, please.
I would pay much more attention to my work if I didn't have to worry about the clothes I wear to work. I like to wear my loose pants and sweatshirts and cannot hardly stand to wear a tie and suit coat. How can I get anything decent done if I am yanking at my collar all day or fighting with the pull of my coat?	**(Group One)** I've read some studies which seem to suggest employees actually work closer to their potential if they have at least one casual dress day a week. Do you think our company might be able to look into incorporating such a plan? **(Group Two)** I would really enjoy my job better if I could come to work in really casual clothes. It is so much easier to concentrate on my projects when I am comfortable. Wouldn't it be nice if all companies had a 'casual Friday'? **(Group Three)** I wish I could wear my favorite clothes to work. If I was comfortable, I would pay more attention to what I was doing and I am sure I would work a whole lot harder than I do all dressed up but yanking at my collar or fighting with the pull of my coat!